Alan Evans demonstrating in April 2019 at Memphis, USA

Cover image: based on The Forge, Arian Leljak
Photo courtesy of the artist

Photo courtesy of Metal Museum Memphis

Earth
Fire
Iron

Alan Evans and the New Iron Age

Edited by George Breeze, Lesley Greene and Mary Greensted
with voices from the artist blacksmith community

QUICK THORN

Earth Fire Iron: Alan Evans and the New Iron Age
© 2025

George Breeze, Lesley Greene and Mary Greensted are hereby identified as the authors of this work in accordance with section 77 of the Copyright, Designs and Patent Act, 1988. They assert and give notice of their moral rights under this Act.

Published by Quickthorn
info@quickthornbooks.com
www.quickthornbooks.com
@quickthornbooks

All rights reserved. No part of this book may be reproduced, stored in a retrieval system or transmitted in any form by any means (electronic or mechanical, through reprography, digital transmission, recording or otherwise) without prior written permission of the publisher.

Every effort has been made to trace the copyright holders and obtain permission to reproduce images in this book. Please do get in touch with any enquiries.

Publisher: Katy Bevan
Project editor: Charlotte Abrahams
Book design: Francesca Chalk

Printed in the UK by Short Run Press, Exeter

Printed on FSC certified paper

British Library Cataloguing in Publication Data applied for
ISBN 9781-7-393160-99

CONTENTS

2   FOREWORD
Sandy Nairne

4   INTRODUCTION
George Breeze

6   GLOSSARY

8   ALAN: A PERSONAL REFLECTION
Lesley Greene

20   PIONEERING CONTINENTAL BLACKSMITHS
Fritz Kühn, Paul Zimmermann, Antonio Benetton, Hermann Gradinger

24   ALAN EVANS WITHIN THE ARTS AND CRAFTS MOVEMENT
Mary Greensted

37   TRADITIONAL BLACKSMITHING – THE PENWITH GATE

38   ARTIST PROFILE – Christoph Friedrich

40   ALAN EVANS AND THE NEW IRON AGE
Peter Parkinson

52   PIONEERING BRITISH BLACKSMITHS
Richard Quinnell, Peter Parkinson, Jim Horrobin, Stuart Hill

56   ST PAUL'S CATHEDRAL GATES
Sandy Nairne

60   ARTIST PROFILE – Sam Pearce

CONTENTS

64	**ALAN EVANS: EARTH, MATERIAL, PRACTICE**	
	Paul Harper	
72	ARTIST PROFILE – Lisa Wisdom	
76	**CONTEMPLATING CARBON**	
	Daniel Carpenter	
82	ARTIST PROFILE – Shona Johnson	
87	**COMMISSIONING**	
	Lucy Quinnell	
96	ARTIST PROFILE – Dane Stevens	
100	**ART SCHOOL FOR BLACKSMITHS**	
	Delyth Done	
107	ARTIST PROFILE – Arian Leljak	
112	ARTIST PROFILE – Melissa Cole	
116	**ALAN EVANS, A SINGULAR VIEW**	
	Matthew Fedden	
118	**FURTHER READING**	

Nailsworth Cycle Fest Handicap W. Ride SNJ Trophy
made and donated by Alan Evans, 7 May 2000

FOREWORD

Sandy Nairne

> *I will not change an error if it feels right, for the error is more human than perfection. I do not seek answers.*
>
> David Smith, *Tradition and Identity*, Ohio University, 17 April 1959

EARTH, FIRE, IRON is a large-scale creative project – an exhibition, publication and programme of activities – with two closely linked purposes: to celebrate the work of the artist blacksmith Alan Evans, who sadly died in 2023, and equally to engage a new generation of artists in the challenges and delights of forging and rendering in iron and steel.

All craft processes arguably require new inspiration and periodic renewal, something well understood by William Morris whose fierce creativity was fuelled and refuelled by British vernacular and medieval traditions, as well as by Icelandic and Asian sources. Many of the sparks that ignited the Arts and Crafts movement were the ideas of John Ruskin, including a close focus on nature and skilled hand-work. But it was Morris and his friends and associates who demonstrated how these ideas could be put into everyday design and practice, in houses, churches and village halls, with determination and skill. Subsequent generations of artists and designers from Charles Rennie Mackintosh to Thomas Heatherwick have continued to develop that creative approach.

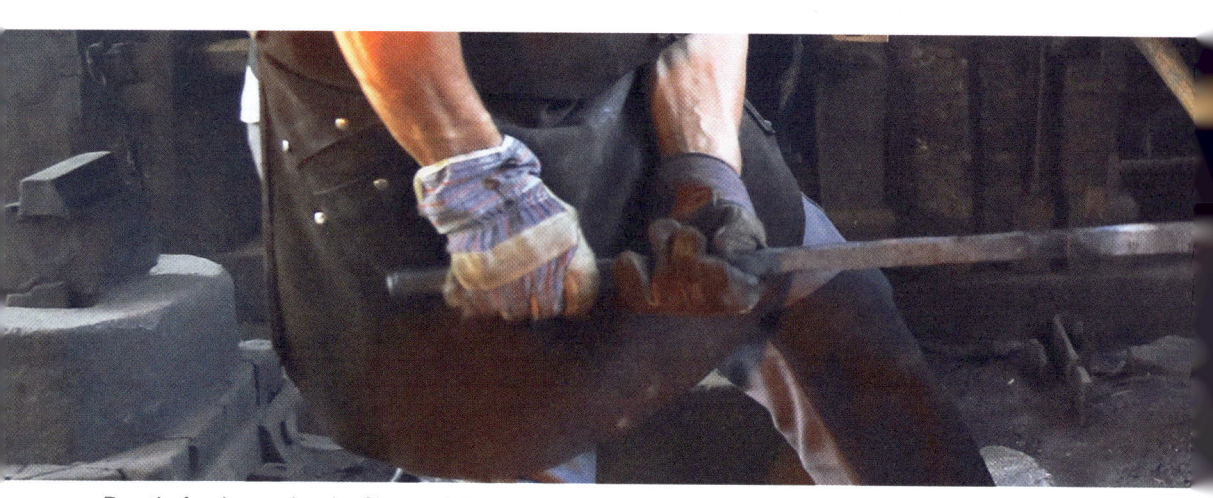

Detail of a photo taken by Christoph Friedrich in his Swiss forge

Blacksmithing has now become recognised as the sophisticated art that it is. But it was not always so, and renewal has come at different points in time. After Amina Chatwin (author of *Into the New Iron Age: Modern British Blacksmiths*, Coach House Publishing, United Kingdom, 1995) participated in the Crafts Council's ground-breaking Forging Iron conference of 1980, she recorded how, 'It all entered our minds like a thunderbolt... It was a revelation... the very air was electric... It is no exaggeration to say that it changed our lives.'

However different metal-working is from painting in terms of material and range of colours, the physical touch of the maker is revealed in the surface of the work in both forms and this leads us, as viewers, to find expression and seek meaning. Like painting, it is an art in which we can delight that error might be, as the American sculptor David Smith put it, 'more human than perfection'. And an art in which we should be reassured by Mackintosh's own motto:

There is hope in honest error, none in the icy perfections of the mere stylist.

I hope that this book and its various contributions will inspire and support new generations of makers, pursuing their own forms of innovation and renewal.

Photo courtesy of Christoph Friedrich

INTRODUCTION

George Breeze

The core of this book commemorates the career of Stroud artist blacksmith Alan Evans (1952–2023), reflecting on his background, work and values as vital forces in the emergence of British artist blacksmithing during the second half of the twentieth century.

In 1994, Quakers in Britain published a powerful little booklet called *Advices and Queries*. Advice number 27 opens with the words 'Live adventurously. When choices arise, do you take the way that offers the fullest opportunity for the use of your gifts in the service of God and the community? Let your life speak'. Alan, a Quaker, would have been aware of this publication in later life, but the vital point is that he lived the advice it contained to the full. Indeed, if a two-word motto could be applied to him it would be 'live adventurously'. It was the Quakers who lent Alan money in 1978 to set up a studio-workshop where he could try out his own ideas in opposition to the traditional orthodoxy of blacksmithing. An excellent draughtsman, he worked tirelessly on original designs and he also shared innovative ideas and freely mentored others in new ways of doing things.

EARTH, FIRE, IRON rightly celebrates Alan's work and legacy, but it goes well beyond that too, as he would have wished. In these pages you will find essays considering the work of some of his contemporaries in what has been called the New Iron Age; the impact of climate change and environmental issues on the craft; how public and private commissioning of artist blacksmiths works in practice and the origins, character and impact of the blacksmithing course at Hereford College of Arts, a key powerhouse in the craft nationally. There are also first-hand stories from seven working artist blacksmiths, four of whom are in mid-career and three who are just starting out in the craft. In short, this book aims to encourage and help

Detail of *'The Lookout'*, collage of found metal by Lisa Wisdom

students, makers and potential clients and inform and inspire all those interested in the crafts in general and artist blacksmithing in particular.

This book would not have come about had not the idea for it originated in an exhibition **EARTH FIRE IRON: Alan Evans and the New Iron Age,** held at the Museum in the Park, Stroud, Gloucstershire, in the autumn of 2025. So our first thanks must be to the enthusiastic team at the Museum and associated Cowle Trust for wholeheartedly embracing the idea and giving space to it in its busy exhibition calendar, especially Kevin Ward and Abigail Large. Their can-do attitude is shared by members of the British Artist Blacksmiths Association (BABA) who have played such a huge and important part in the project, providing both ideas and practical support, led by Andy Rowe and Shona Johnson. The support of Richard Quinnell, who started BABA and is a fund of knowledge as to where Alan's works are and where answers to difficult questions can be found, runs like a river through the whole process in both the exhibition and this book. Delyth Done, who heads up the blacksmithing course at Hereford College of Arts and is an influential figure in the field, has been extremely generous with her time. We are, of course, grateful to Sandy Nairne for writing the Foreword and to all the writers for their thoughtful contributions and keenness to support the whole concept of the book, as are the publishers, Quickthorn under the leadership of Katy Bevan and her editor Charlotte Abrahams.

As ideas for the exhibition grew, so did thoughts for what this book should contain, so the financial support underpinning the former has enabled the latter to be a long-term benefit of the thinking behind the exhibition. Chief among this support is Arts Council England.

Photo Lisa Wisdom

GLOSSARY

A QUICK GUIDE TO KEY BLACKSMITHING TERMS

A blacksmith is a metalworker using iron or steel.

A forge is both the blacksmith's fire and their workplace.

An anvil is a large block of cast or forged steel with a flattened top on which the blacksmith works/hammers the heated metal.

Fire needs fuel, oxygen and heat to keep burning. Blacksmiths traditionally have used charcoal, coal or coke as their fuel source. At its most basic, oxygen comes from blowing on a fire. From medieval times bellows made of wood and leather have been used to direct a stream of air to the base of the fire and enabled the flames to get hot enough to melt iron. Forge blowers, introduced in the twentieth century, are typically powered by electricity and can supply a constant supply of oxygen and air to the blacksmith's fire. Today, blacksmiths are experimenting with hand-cranked bellows – not dissimilar to a large fan hair dryer – and a handle as a more environmentally friendly way of pumping air into the fire.

Blacksmiths use a variety of metals based on steel, which is an alloy of iron and carbon. Mild steel, the most commonly used material, contains only a very small amount of carbon – less than 0.25%. This makes it more malleable and easier to weld. Cast iron is steel containing up to 4% carbon and has a relatively low melting temperature. It is the most common ferrous metal used for large constructions. Wrought iron is a historic material, no longer produced, but available as a salvaged material. It is an almost chemically pure form of iron that was mixed with silica slag.

Blacksmiths work by shaping or striking their material with a hammer. **Water-powered hammers** driven by water wheels are rare today. **Power hammers** were introduced in the 1880s and use an electrical or steam power source to raise a mechanical hammer and bring it down at speed onto the piece being worked.

Welding is the process of joining two pieces of a particular metal, using the same metal. (As distinct from soldering, which joins two pieces, using a different metal.)

Fire or forge welding is the ancient blacksmithing technique of heating two pieces in the fire until the surface is essentially molten and bringing them into intimate contact with a few smart blows, to achieve a joint. **Electric arc welding** uses the heat of an electric arc (a continuous spark) to melt the surface of the two pieces of metal to be joined and a rod or wire of the same metal to provide the joint material. Arc welding was developed during the First World War and is now commonplace. Today it can be achieved by manual, semi-automated or fully automated methods. **Manual arc welding** uses an electrode rod or stick with its core acting as the joint material. It is a versatile technique, ideal for repair work, and relatively inexpensive, but weld times are rather slow.

Gas tungsten arc welding is also a manual method and requires more skill. It is good for welding thin materials and producing high-quality finishes. **Semi-automated** or **automated arc welding** relies on an electric arc from an AC or DC power supply, creating an intense heat of around 6,500°F (3,600°C) which melts the metal.

ALAN: A PERSONAL REFLECTION

Lesley Greene

Photo courtesy of Lesley Greene

Alan Evans with his dog, Poppy on the Isle of Arran, 2015

The ring of the hammer, the song of the anvil, the medley of new forms forged from conversations in different languages and across visual cultures. This was the new language artist blacksmiths shared in the late 1970s and 1980s, energising exciting ideas that led to a renaissance in artist blacksmithing.

Making, 'waste not, want not', and the family legacy of grandparents and parents committed to what was – and still is – considered an alternative lifestyle, formed Alan's ethics, values, life and work. Living simply, living sustainably, were core concerns. His work reflects that, but simplicity is not achieved without a hard thought-out process of defining a moment in iron in the precise touch of the master smith. As the economist E. F. Schumacher wrote in his book *Small Is Beautiful: Economics as if People Mattered*, (Blond & Briggs 1973, Harper Collins 2010–present), 'Any third-rate engineer or researcher can increase complexity; but it takes a certain flair of real insight to make things simple again.'

THE CHALLENGES OF DESIGN AND DRAWINGS

Drawing is the beginning of design, the 'scent' of an idea, the essence of what might be – the way in which an artist observes and sees both what is there and what is not.

The challenge for the traditional British blacksmith was that, until the early 1970s, the design was made for him (and it was usually a 'he') to copy, or at the most choose from, standard patterns. Technically, there was training that facilitated the use of the hammer and the teasing out of the liveliness of a traditional coil, but as for an overall design, that was provided by standard pattern books.

Drawing has always been an essential part of the artist's work. It is one of the best means of observation; life drawing is the foundation of art school training. Drawing is not just the observation of something to develop, whether it be a landscape or a figure, but an exploration enabling the sketching out of ideas. It is the notebook for thoughts and dreams, and without the necessity of an end result or a commissioned constraint, it allows for impulse, imagination, improvisation and discovery; creativity in essence. And drawings are art in their own right.

The blacksmith's 'trade' has been – and still is – generally tied to commissions. For the artist blacksmith to develop his or her identity as an artist, the drawing is an integral part of the design and the design development process. The design of any work can only benefit from the expression that drawings bring to the heart of things. For the commissioned blacksmith, acknowledging and valuing the drawings that are the imaginative process towards a design is critical. There should be a context and recompense for this. The artist blacksmith – often, like any artist, driven by commissions – needs to make time to reflect and refresh and to challenge themselves about the quality of their work. Time out drawing is time out to do just this.

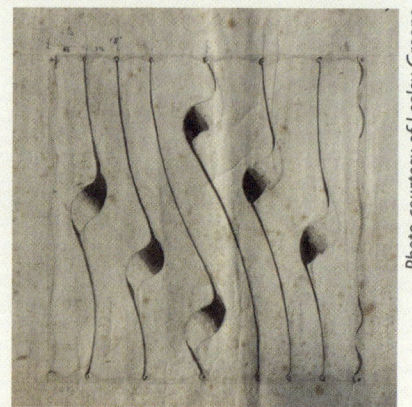

Photo courtesy of Lesley Greene

Drawing by Alan Evans

Photo Alan Evans

'Gate Gate' by Alan Evans, 1981

Alan was clear that jewellery was his craft but blacksmithing his art. He believed that to fulfil their potential the artist must follow their work, be true to themselves and not aim for financial or career success. He loved new technologies – he always drew (when I was working, he was drawing) and was the first of his contemporaries to use a computer to draw. He mended all the computers at home too, taking them apart and putting them together on the kitchen table, and was among one of the first blacksmiths to exploit the potential of the power hammer. Alan had an inner declaration of purpose. He said he was 'driven... I did not have a choice in the matter,

ALAN: A PERSONAL REFLECTION

and what mattered most was having the opportunity to create.' Alan was lucky to be alive at a time when there was a renaissance in blacksmithing and a combination of circumstances that created a wide interest in artist blacksmithing.

> ## DAVID SMITH
> ## (1906–1965)
>
> © 1968 Thames & Hudson, All rights reserved. This drawing is in the archives of American Art R 3 F 1184 Notebook 36
>
> David Smith *'Studies for Personages and Tanktotems'* pencil, 1952
>
> Smith was an American abstract expressionist who had a significant influence on some British blacksmiths. Inspired by European artists, such as Picasso and Gonzalez and trained as an engineer and welder, he became a prolific sculptor pioneering the use of welded steel in his art: 'Since I worked in factories and made automobile parts I saw a chance to make sculpture in the tradition I was already rooted in,' he wrote in his book, *David Smith by David Smith: Sculpture and Writings,* edited by Cleve Gray (Thames and Hudson, 1968). Over his lifetime, Smith created an astonishingly varied range of work from monumental, geometric, abstract work to fine drawings and figurative sculpture. He began much of his work with a found object '...sometimes when I am sweeping the floor and I stumble across a few parts and that sets me off thinking… ,' as he put it in his book *(ibid)*. Some of his most important sculptures are the 'Tanktotem' series that resemble figures or 'personages'. In 1962, the Italian government invited Smith to develop work for the *Festival of Two Worlds* in Spoleto. He set up a studio in an abandoned welding factory in the town of Voltri where, bringing together the scrap metal with found objects such as tongs, tools and carts, he produced nearly 30 sculptures in as many days. The *Voltri* series seem to become, like his tanktotems, figures walking a landscape.

Alan did not wholly reject tradition. His knowledge of traditional techniques was the basis from which he forged a new aesthetic, at the same time as he was inspired by the energy of European blacksmithing – among them the Kühns, the Zimmermann family, Italian sculptor and metalworker Toni Benetton (who we met in Treviso), and metal sculptors here and abroad. I have a photograph of him deep in discussion with Philip King at the British Artist Blacksmiths Association's (BABA) conference at West Surrey College of Art and Design (now the University College of Art and Design Farnham), for example; he was the only blacksmith to attend the Spanish

Photo courtesy of Lesley Greene

Alan Evans, Garden Gate, Ledbury. Private commission. Chop and twist technique, 1990/91

sculptor, Eduardo Chillida's talk at the Dublin International Sculpture conference in 1988. Alan, no doubt like many smiths, spent hours mulling over and pulling together forged oddments, bits and pieces lying on the workshop floor, experimenting with assemblages. He had intense periods of slicing zig-zag forms from tube, exploring the possibilities of creating new life from industrial iron.

Arguably, Alan caught the tradition at its best and – with that knowledge and the inventiveness that came from his left handedness, an enquiring mind and an aesthetic intelligence – made it anew. His thinking was encouraged by Anthony Caro, who spoke in one lecture of the three significances of sculpture being 'scale, scale, scale', and what Chillida termed the 'space between', referring to the breathing space left by the removal of an object being as important as the material 'containing' it. Maybe Alan had Smith's 'sentinels' – watchful figures in a landscape – somewhere in mind when he paid homage to Benneton (1910–1966) with his piece 'Toni totem'.

> *'We waste fewer of the earth's energy and material resources if they are used well. If the design of the piece is good enough it will speak to those in the future and… unlike fashion will not need to be recycled.'*
>
> (Quote from Alan Evans' presentation at the University of East Anglia Obscure Objects of Desire Conference, 10–12 January 1997, organised by Tanya Harrod under the auspices of the UEA Fellowship in Critical Appreciation in the Crafts and Design)

Alan's interest in the environment was as a direct result of a particular upbringing and a commitment. He was educated at the Sibford School in Banbury, Oxfordshire where the Quaker education included art, music, metal and woodwork. So many of his pieces reflect the local landscape; even large commissions interrogate a bird, an animal or were even, as in the railings he made in London's Broadgate, inspired by the jabiru stork. His father's practice of using locally grown, seasoned timber influenced the use of local timber in his seats. His street lighting designs did not cause night sky pollution. Materials were sparingly forged. Cycle racks were cleverly and efficiently cantilevered off one support (rather than many), and he insisted on re-use when he could. Amongst many projects, he found an inventive way to use an RSJ for the Royal Society of Arts pollution abatement award in 1983, and incorporated old tracks belonging to Great Western Railway for the Railway Triangle commission 'Trackworks' in 2019 in Gloucester. Invention was part of the repertoire – bars spread and divided with the power hammer; twists made with the help of the bench-vice, then spread again in an opposite direction and forged down the rest of the bar. (Spread elements suspend the shorter lengths, with batwing-like shapes used at either end for hinges and catches for a handle and latch.)

Alan had a strongly held conviction that a life of low consumption makes a positive contribution to society by way of example. The maker's life is not escapism but a form of dissidence; it challenges our norms in the best way that it can. 'Living to work' rather than 'working to live', he said. He was proud of his dissident background (grandfather Basil, a conscientious objector, was imprisoned in WW1) and championed the crafts and the importance of design quality intrinsic to the best of all makers.

Photo Alan Evans with the permission of the owners

Brimpsfield House gate latch

He stood up for the crafts in all ways, always opened the workshop and shared his home to many young smiths. Committed to equality and fair pay, he always paid as he trained and mentored – and many of his apprentices repaid him by working as part of his team on some of his large commissions. His social role was integral to working in the public realm – and for him giving high-quality artist blacksmithing a public visibility and accessibility was critically important. Alan forged the iron to be inviting to our touch – you *feel* the marks of the hammer in his work, the magic of a gate latch is instinctively natural – and in every piece, the intention of the maker supports a deceptive simplicity and warmth of form.

His work was always one-off, made on his own terms. He refused to make to someone else's design and he never let any piece of work out of his studio until it was wholly acceptable to him, even if he lost money on the project. He enjoyed working with other artists – with Sue Ridge on Southampton station and David Poston on St Hugh's Shrine in Lincoln Cathedral. He was always a member of BABA, involved in its events, often on its committees and chaired the Association for two years.

Personal interests are reflected in his work. Puns, crosswords, music, numbers and words reference the making, meeting and playfulness of pieces – 'Gate Gate', '24 Pine Hill', 'Reflect', 'Trackworks', 'Go Between', 'Communication' – the latter a piece without any welding or fixing, simply a balancing of all the elements.

The BABA touring exhibition *Fe* in 1994 offered Alan the opportunity to make a work sing. This piece is 'Ring the Changes', played by Evelyn Glennie at the exhibition opening. In his introduction to the catalogue 'Touching the Senses', William Kirby wrote that 'Ring the Changes' '...not only had its own voice' (a voice modulated by the way the participant played it) '...but by the linearity of its design... the ideal combination of designing the sound as an intrinsic element in the line and the "iron-ness" of the piece.'

We are ringing the changes again, it is time to make new music, and Alan would have applauded this new iron age.

Photo courtesy of Lesley Greene

The Craftsmen of Gloucestershire group photo, 1980s. Alan is sitting cross-legged in the front row. These were professional crafts people who sourced their living entirely from their craft

ALAN: A PERSONAL REFLECTION

Working on the project 'Go Between' 1990–91. Screen Broadgate Development, City of London. Commissioned by RoseHaugh Stanhope

Welding the Cross for Christ the King Ecumenical Church, Milton Keynes, 1991

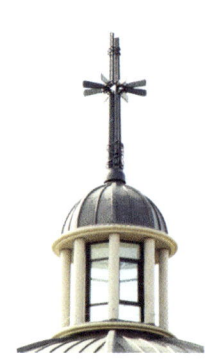

Cross, Ecumenical Church, Milton Keynes, 1991

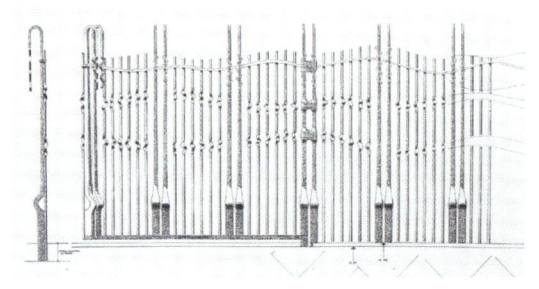

Design for the barriers at the Broadgate Development, London

Bench, Steel and Oak, High Wycombe, 1997

Cycle 'bollards', Churchill Gardens, Cheltenham, c2000

Alan at the anvil in his forge at Whiteway

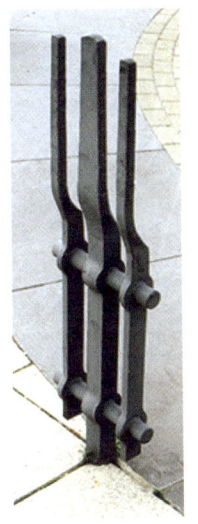

Railings, commissioned by the Public Record Office, Kew, 1992

Part of a commission for Holy Trinity Church, Brompton, London, 1986–7

Steel, wood and fabric screen by Sue Ridge and Alan Evans for St George's Cathedral, London, 1989

Stages in the process of forging the PATAS Trophy, 1983

Toni Totem, 1991–2

Alan at the power hammer, Ratho Byres 'Forge-In' 2022 in honour of Phil Johnson

Alan's Masterclass Museum of Metalwork Memphis workshop, with participant Elizabeth Belz, 2019

EARTH FIRE IRON 17

EDUARDO CHILLIDA
(1924–2002)

Chillida trained in architecture before he worked with a local blacksmith in San Sebastián, Spain. He won the Grand Prix at the Venice Biennale in 1958 for his work in the Spanish Pavilion, establishing his international reputation. Chillida was relatively little known in the United Kingdom (the artist and historian Roland Penrose gave him an exhibition in London in 1965) until he gave the keynote talk in 1988 at the 'year of sculpture' at the International Conference on Sculpture held in Trinity College, Dublin. Alan Evans attended this lecture.

Chillida's approach to sculpture was through drawing – 'I draw a lot... I don't try to do drawings in the normal sense, they are working material ...but I try to find the spirit of the work... the scent of the work... connected to the spirit of the work I am going to do', he explained in the catalogue to his 1990 exhibition, *Chillida* at the Hayward Gallery, London. He was a prolific artist, producing collages, drawings and low reliefs throughout his working career. Writing in the Hayward exhibition catalogue, Penrose described his drawings of hands as grasping 'firmly a handful of space' and 'hands that grasp an idea'. Chillida's sculptures are in a sense amazing landscapes within which inner spaces are created by the heavy weight of gravity.

Chillida's public artworks, such as the commission for the UNESCO building in Paris, have an immense presence. He welcomed local commissions that include, The Combs of the Wind, a homage to San Sebastián and the local coast where grew up. He worked closely with his local foundry, which produced most of his large public commissions.

courtesy of Sucesión Chillida

Eduardo Chillida, Espacios Perforados II, 1952

SIR ANTHONY CARO
(1924–2013)

Caro trained at the Royal Academy Schools, London and became an assistant to Henry Moore. In 1963 he had a major exhibition at the Whitechapel Art Gallery in London where he showed assemblages of abstract steel sculpture on the floor of the gallery into and around which the public could move. This access and interaction was a radical departure from traditional sculpture on plinths. He became the twentieth century's leading British sculptor, making works from a huge variety of materials, including iron that incorporated found metal objects such as tools, as well as rusted steel, bronze, soft and roll-edge steel and brightly painted steel.

Caro taught for many years at St Martins School of Art (now Central Saint Martins University of the Arts London) and lectured extensively, influencing a generation of artists. It was at one of Caro's lectures that Alan Evans first heard him say, 'There are three things of importance for sculpture – scale, scale, scale.' It was a phrase that stuck with Alan and he quoted it often.

Sir Anthony Caro OM CBE, Early One Morning, (1962)

Courtesy of Anthony Caro Centre

EARTH FIRE IRON

PIONEERING CONTINENTAL BLACKSMITHS

Amina Chatwin's now historical 'bible' on modern blacksmithing Into the New Iron Age: Modern British Blacksmiths, *Coach House Publishing, United Kingdom, 1995, suggests that the 'new beginning of creative ironwork' in Britain was the International Conference on Forging Iron in 1980, held at Hereford Technical College. American and continental smiths attended the conference. Of those, the following were particularly influential and are mentioned in this publication.*

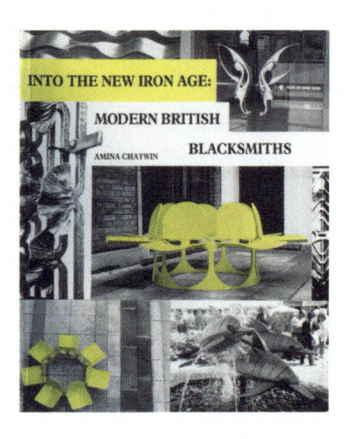

The cover of Amina Chatwin's pioneering book,
'Into the New Iron Age, Modern British Blacksmiths', 1995

FRITZ KÜHN
(EAST GERMANY 1910–1967)

Kühn remains one of the most hugely respected and early innovators in forged iron. He was born in Berlin into a metalworking family, completed his master craftsman certificate in 1937 and founded his studio forge as an artist blacksmith. By the 1950s, he described himself as an Artist Craftsman. His technical knowledge of the material stimulated his imagination and enabled him to be creative and experimental. Kühn was inspired by nature but particularly by Karl Blossfeld's black and white photographic images of the forms and patterns of plants. Kühn published numerous specialist and art books and his work and his many commissions inspired European artist blacksmiths and the emerging British blacksmiths. His son, Achim Kühn attended and demonstrated at the 1980 Hereford Technical College Conference.

Fritz Kühn Catalogue *Arbeiten in Stahl Und Metal*' Screen designed for the East German Pavilion 1958 World Exhibition in Brussels and and exhibited in Lindau, 1980

ANTONIO (TONI) BENETTON
(ITALY 1910–1996)

Benetton attended the British Artist Blacksmiths Association (BABA) 1980 conference in Hereford with his son Simon, with whom he made sculpture. Toni Benetton lived in Treviso and set up an Academy of Iron (Accademia del Ferro), leading courses and teaching there. He created large-sized outdoor sculptures, often figurative and of animals and birds, and set up one of Italy's first outdoor sculpture parks in the process. He participated in many international sculpture events, including the 1986 Venice Biennale. His work typically involved slicing iron plate into thin sections or ribbons, thus allowing light to penetrate the material. This is one key characteristic of his work. One of his sculptures, 'Estensionne', was bought by the Victoria and Albert Museum in 1982. It is a flat piece of Corten steel, twisted and with a curved triangular steel top sheet cut into ribbons. The Museo Toni Benetton, based in the province of Treviso in part of the premises of Villa Marignana, was founded in 2000 by the Benetton family to display his work.

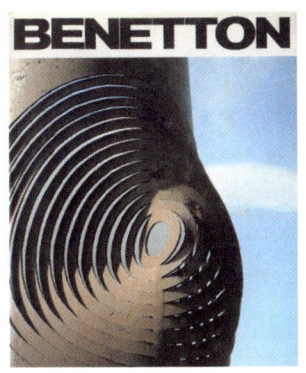

Front cover of *Benetton Il Ferro*, published by the Provincia di Treviso 1991 showing 'Il Cerchio' ('The Circle'), 1982

PIONEERING CONTINENTAL BLACKSMITHS

HERMANN GRADINGER

Gradinger trained as a locksmith, then took the Master Craftsman's Certificate. From the mid-1960s, his work became widely recognised for its precision and design quality. He exhibited his works at various venues, including Lindau, Bremen, Aachen, Munich, Paris, London and New York and he was one of the first four internationally renowned smiths to be invited to the inaugural BABA conference in Hereford. He generally worked to commission. His views on the critical relationship between design and making influenced the aesthetic of several emerging British blacksmiths. For a number of years, Gradinger was federal chairman of the Metalworking and Design Group in the Federal Association for the Metal Sector where his opinions on technique and design were powerfully made: 'The design, the fabrication and the achievement of an excellent result are all inextricably linked,' he writes on his website, 'our work ethos doesn't require technical standards but simply the satisfaction of creating high-quality products. Compliance with a technical standard says nothing meaningful about the quality of a design… To reach the source of the river, man must swim against the tide.'

From 'Kunst aus Dem' published by Julius Hoffman, Verlag Stuttgart

Gradinger, *Forged Friendship*, sculpture in forged steel for twin towns, 1986

PAUL ZIMMERMANN

Zimmermann worked with his wife, Ruth, in the small German town of Pliezhausen, and is considered one of the first German blacksmiths to create innovative and contemporary designs in the field of traditional blacksmithing. Integral to his concerns as an artist blacksmith is the inspiration of nature and the surfaces that are an important design element in his work. The surface traces are heated and annealed to be touched and felt. 'It should always be evident where a gate is to be touched', he said in his monograph, *Atelier Zimmermann: Ironworks,* Winifried Sturzl, Hartmann Books, 2019. The sensitivity in his work comes from an awareness that iron outlives us and is a legacy, the design of which is 'an obligation to us' and 'what we leave behind will be the witness of today's craftsmanship to our descendants.' (*ibid*) German grave markers are often made from iron and many of Zimmermann's commissions are for memorials. He taught in many workshops in Europe and the USA, and generously shared his art and philosophy that 'shape is limitation – design is disclosure.' His works are characterised by a refined and simple aesthetic that he has explored throughout his life. 'I do not seek anything decorative – rather silence and calmness,' he said. Of their three children, two are blacksmiths. Heiner Zimmermann continues in his father's tradition and is now professor of metalwork at Gothenburg University.

Photo Paul Zimmermann

Zimmermann, candle holder, 1998

ALAN EVANS WITHIN THE ARTS AND CRAFTS MOVEMENT

Mary Greensted

Metalworking crafts were among the most important developments ever made by humankind. During the Iron Age in Europe, it became possible to produce stronger tools and weapons in larger quantities. Both iron, and iron smelted to form steel, have enabled generations of ingenious blacksmiths to forge pieces that were both useful and decorative. Working for other craftsmen, farmers and the local community, they combined craft skills with engineering and design.

Alfred Bucknell with his son, Norman, in their forge at Waterlane, Gloucestershire, early 1930s

The art of the blacksmith flourished in continental Europe during the Renaissance with many skilled makers coming to Britain from the time of Henry VIII onwards. Jean Tijou, a French Hugenot, came in the early eighteenth century during the reign of William and Mary to make gates and screens for the gardens of Hampton Court, as well as ironwork in the choir of St Paul's Cathedral in London and the gates of the

Clarendon Building, Oxford. He also published a book of his designs in 1693 which featured baroque motifs such as scrolling foliage and elaborate flower forms in sheet metal attached to the iron structure. The eighteenth-century gates at Erddig House, the National Trust property near Wrexham, by the Davis brothers are typical of this type of work. Traditional craftsmen – furniture makers, plasterers as well as smiths and other metalworkers – became increasingly reliant on pattern books for their designs which offered a simple selection process for their customers. In the long term however, this way of working did stifle individual creativity. The quarterly number of the Rural Industries Bureau's magazine in the spring of 1927 criticised 'too much attention... given to slavish copies of antique specimens' because of the maker's over-anxiety to add ornament rather than consider proportion, refinement of form and efficiency.

Photo courtesy of Mary Greensted

The door at St Mary's, an Anglo-Saxon church at Deerhurst, Gloucestershire

Writing in the summer of 1949, the artist and devoted chronicler of Cotswold crafts, Freda Derrick wanted to convince her readers of the absolute value of the country workmen. In her book, *A Trinity of Craftsmen* (Chapman & Hall, London, 1950) she wrote, 'They may look small from a distance; but if you get close to them, you will have a better measure of their greatness.' Derrick visited a Gloucestershire smithy where a single family had worked for at least four generations. One brother had branched out to more decorative work, repairing the gates of big houses and making weather vanes that were inspired by an old-fashioned, black Malacca cock that ran about the forge. He related how, 'I put him up on the bench, and sketched him.' There were always some traditional craftsmen eager to develop their own designs.

Photo © The Guild of Handicraft Trust and Court Barn, Chipping Campden

Blacksmiths at the Guild of Handicrafts, Chipping Campden, 1906

To some extent, the situation in Gloucestershire was slightly different. It is hard to credit this today, but the Cotswold countryside was considered unattractive and unfashionable in the nineteenth century. Most of the land was divided up into large estates whose owners preferred to live and spend their wealth elsewhere. Towns such as Chipping Campden in the north of the county, and Winchcombe, Painswick, Lechlade and Fairford further south reflected something of the area's former glory as the centre of the wool trade but there were also rundown villages and hamlets and real examples of rural poverty. Many old customs connected with the crafts, however, had survived in a way that they hadn't closer to London and other cities. This, together with the availability of cheap land and accommodation and the advent of the railways, brought potential new artistic and idealistic settlers to the area, including the Whiteway Colony where Alan Evans was born.

The philosophy of the Colony, based on the rejection of private property in favour of communal self-help, was developed by a number of Christian Socialists based in Croydon, South London, inspired by accounts of collective life on Leo Tolstoy's Russian country estate. A commune was set up at Purleigh, Essex, but after a disagreement, a breakaway group moved to Gloucestershire. The move was spearheaded and enabled by Samuel Bracher, originally from Gloucester, who had inherited £1,000. In 1898, he used these funds to purchase 41 acres of rough upland pasture at Whiteway, near Miserden and, on completion of the sale, the title deeds were burned in a ceremonious rejection of the idea of property. (Interestingly, the community's contribution to the millenium was a flaming torch made by Alan, *see p35*.) Among the early members who made the journey from Purleigh to Whiteway by bicycle – a distance of some 150 miles – were Nellie Shaw, a dressmaker specialising in artistic and rational dress for the middle classes, and Arnold Eiloart, a chemistry teacher from Denmark.

The colonists struggled to live off the land. The Arts and Crafts architect, C. R. Ashbee, visited Whiteway in 1904. Two years earlier, he had uprooted his Guild of Handicraft – some 50 craftsmen and their families – from London's East End to the nearby town of Chipping Campden to realise his conviction that the crafts would thrive in the countryside. He and the two guildsmen who accompanied him had long talks with some of the colonists and he noted in his Journals for September 1904 (King's College Archives, Cambridge):

> *We found here people who seem to be back to the land in grim earnest... all very uncouth and experimental. In the cabins are pianos, books, machine-made chairs and tables and other of the incrementa of civilisation, protesting as it were against this half-hearted return to barbarism.*

Closer to Ashbee's aesthetic sensibilities were the designer-architects, Ernest Gimson and Sidney Barnsley, who had moved to the south Cotswolds from London in 1893. As students, they had been involved in the Arts and Crafts movement taking shape initially in the capital and other big cities, but the desire to live close to nature and practise what W. R. Lethaby, A. H. Powell and F. L. Griggs in their book, *Ernest Gimson, His Life & Work* (Stratford-on-Avon, 1924), termed 'good handicrafts and building' inspired them to choose a rural setting. Sidney's elder brother, Ernest, along with his wife and two daughters, joined them the following year and they settled near the village of Sapperton, six miles from Cirencester. Alongside their architectural work, they made turned ladderback chairs, oak furniture and plasterwork. They also lived a simple life with few of the amenities available to their contemporaries, but enough funds to have solid and tasteful surroundings. There is no record of Gimson or either of the Barnsley brothers visiting Whiteway but, there were links: the woodworker Fred Foster, who designed and made furniture at Whiteway until his death in 1968, spent a short but influential time in Sidney Barnsley's workshop at Sapperton in about 1910.

By the 1920s, the crafts were seen as the way forward at Whiteway. Some of the colonists, spearheaded by Bea Adams, sought out established makers to develop new skills. Bea, who had moved to the Colony from Leicester with her husband Ted in 1906, was an enterprising character. She supplemented their income by taking in paying guests before visiting the Holt Colony, near Cromer in Norfolk with her two daughters to learn leatherwork. She encouraged makers from Holt to visit Whiteway to share their skills and a number of them ended up staying permanently. They became part of the newly-established Cotswold Co-operative of Handicrafts and were joined by other colonists working in a variety of crafts attracted to Whiteway by its ethos and character.

Photo courtesy of Whiteway Archives

Basil Robert at Whiteway instructing Rosemary Randolph and Dedee Morand, 1920s

The craftsmen and women of the Whiteway Colony, particularly the Cotswold Co-operative Handicrafts and the Dodo Press, had links with the local Arts and Crafts movement and took part in exhibitions of Cotswold Art and Craftsmanship that were staged almost annually through the late 1920s and 1930s in Chipping Campden, Cheltenham and Painswick. The leatherworkers Mary and Basil Robert, who had moved to Whiteway from Holt and played an important role in the colony's craft scene, were regular exhibitors. Their daughter Joy, whose character and approach had been shaped by a Forest School and Steiner education, trained as a nurse at the Royal Free Hospital in London and worked at the Cotswold Sanitorium in Cranham, but she was also a maker; predominantly a woodcarver. She married Peter Evans who, after a period working with the Rural Industries Bureau, also decided to take up a craft and went to work for a year with the furniture maker Oliver Morel in rural Herefordshire, near the Welsh border.

(Oliver, a Quaker and a conscientious objector, like many of the Whiteway colonists, had close links with the Cotswold Arts and Crafts movement and ended his working life in Gloucestershire. He had trained with Sidney Barnsley's son Edward in Hampshire before moving to the Welsh borders.) Evans' time there learning from Morel was a formative experience that shaped both his style and approach to furniture making. Both Joy and their baby daughter Rosalind accompanied him, which must have been a challenge, as the living conditions were very primitive – there was no running water or electricity. Their son, the blacksmith Alan Evans, was born back at Whiteway a few years later.

There was no blacksmithing at Whiteway until much later but there were smiths working as part of Ashbee's Guild of Handicraft in London from 1890. Four of them moved with the Guild to Chipping Campden making railings, fire screens, fire tools and firedogs, candlesticks, bell pulls, handles and window latches. Their work was typical of the more artistic work of the period – serviceable and plainer than high Victorian design but with extended curves reminiscent of continental Art Nouveau. It is not clear how much input Ashbee had, but there is no evidence that he produced individual designs for their everyday work. After the Guild of Handicraft folded in 1907, two of the blacksmiths, Bill Thornton and Charley Downer, stayed on and continued working together through the 1930s. Downer left to make aircraft parts in the Lockheed factory at Leamington Spa during the Second World War but Thornton continued forging small-scale pieces until 1947.

Firedog in polished steel, designed by Ernest Gimson and made probably by Alfred Bucknell, about 1905–10

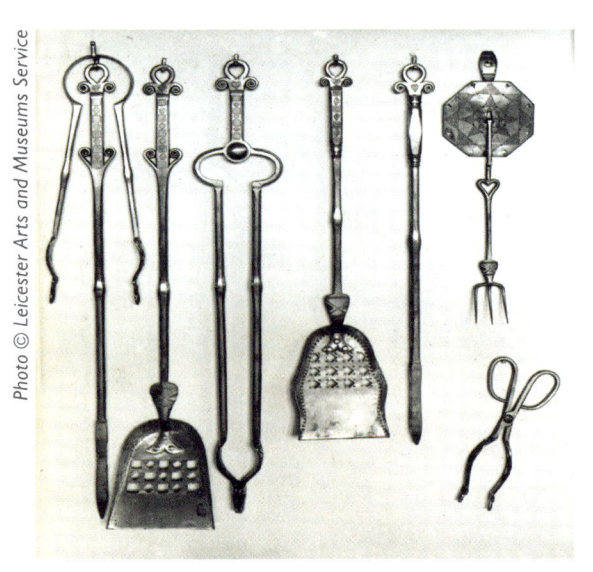

Fire tools in steel designed by Ernest Gimson, 1905–17

In the south Cotswolds, Sidney Barnsley designed and made furniture from 1894 and occasionally turned brass drop handles on a lathe for his pieces. As a student, Ernest Gimson had studied and admired medieval metalwork – gates, fire furniture and the decorative strap hinges on church doors. His first attempts at designing metalwork were for Stoneywell, the house that he built for his elder brother in the Charnwood Forest, Leicestershire. Most of the furniture for the house was commissioned from the Barnsley brothers, but Gimson designed a pair of firedogs and a floor-standing candlestick made for him by John Mace, a blacksmith working in the nearby village of Daglingworth. Gimson seems to have been satisfied with the results, but Mace, a family man in his 40s, was probably not keen to take on regular and challenging work from Gimson. A major commission in 1902 from John Crichton-Stuart, fourth Marquess of Bute, who was renovating the Old Place at Mochrum, a hunting lodge in south-west Scotland, led to Gimson's meeting with Alfred Bucknell, the young and talented son of the blacksmith and wheelwright working in the nearby village of Waterlane in Gloucestershire. The basic hinges and handles made by Alfred met with Gimson's approval. He set up a smithy in Sapperton, and employed Bucknell and subsequently two or three other young smiths to make useful and beautiful domestic metalwork to his design. The relationship between the designer and the makers was close – Gimson would visit the smithy on a daily basis and discuss his designs with the craftsmen. When the architect Philip Webb, a close friend of both William Morris and Ernest Gimson, commented enthusiastically on the beauty of a pair of firedogs exhibited in London in 1907, Ernest replied in a letter dated 23 December, 1907, 'The firedogs were made by the young village smith & were pierced and chased on his anvil. My smiths all think such things rather trivial & are much happier with their forges & hammers – as who wouldn't be!' (The letter is now in the collections of The Wilson, Emery Walker Library.)

Some years after the collapse of the Guild of Handicraft, Ashbee visited Ernest Gimson in the smithy and was shown a pair of iron fire clippers. He noted their conversation in his Journals for May 1914, kept in the archives of King's College, Cambridge. Gimson asked him: 'Can any smith of yours make a piece like that? Oh yes, you may well pour over it – it's the most difficult double joint you can forge.' Gimson regularly discussed issues of both technique and design with his craftsmen and revelled in the technical excellence of the metalwork they produced. Two years later, at the 1916 Arts and Crafts Exhibition held at the Royal Academy in London, a reviewer writing in the volume 29 edition of *Burlington Magazine*, November 1916, described a set of fire irons designed by Gimson and made by Alfred Bucknell as 'modern masterpieces of their kind'. What contemporary blacksmiths appreciate about Gimson's approach to the craft are the technical achievements and the refined touches in the design. As well as the double joint on the fire clippers, all the fire tools fit comfortably in the hand and are beautifully balanced to carry out the job for which they were intended. Decoration was restrained, based on simple curves, cut-outs and punched patterns. A pair of firedogs in polished steel with two bold bow-like curves on the upright are especially striking.

Alfred Bucknell's son, Norman, worked alongside his father from 1930 – his final forge before his death in 2006 was attached to his home in Bisley, not far from Whiteway. He was part of the wider craft community, together with the Evans family, and Alan was both familiar with and appreciative of his, and particularly his father's and Gimson's, work from an early age. When in 1989 he was commissioned to produce a dramatic grille for the newly extended Cheltenham Art Gallery and Museum (now The Wilson), Alan included some discreet references to Gimson's work – a plate in aluminium bronze featuring a squirrel nibbling an acorn echoes Gimson's design for the roundels of a pair of firedogs in the museum's collections. Alan's piece also includes aluminium bronze nuts in the shape of acorns that lock the grille together as an additional reference to Gimson's design.

Gimson's drawing for firedog roundels

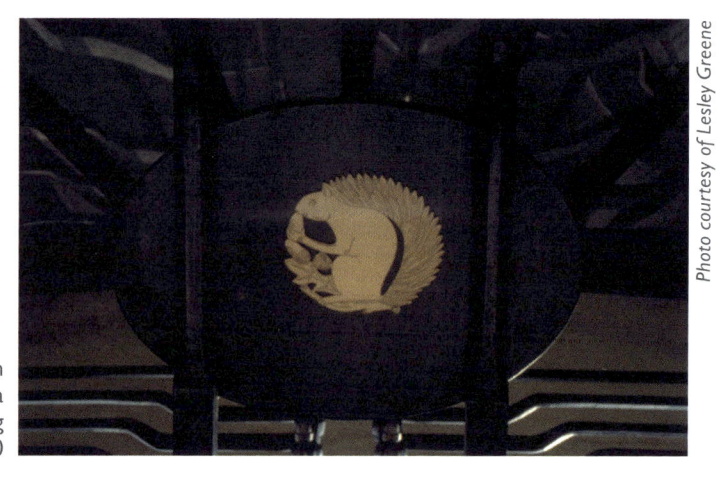

Detail of a wrought iron grille by Alan Evans with a brass squirrel paying homage to Gimson, 1990

Photo © Jeff Buck, Creative Commons Licence

Early eighteenth-century gates at Erddig Park, Wrexham, Wales, restored by Alan Knight with Alan Evans in 1975

Alan's first real experience of the craft however, came from Alan Knight, another blacksmith inspired by Gimson and the Arts and Crafts traditions of the Cotswolds. Born in Birmingham in 1911, Knight was also the son of a talented cabinet maker, although his father had died when he was very young. His mother encouraged him to take up metalworking and he served his apprenticeship with George Bossum at Blackgate forge in north Devon. He then spent two years on the continent, including a period working with the great German smith, Fritz Kühn, before setting up his own forge at Lickey, on the south-western outskirts of Birmingham. He served in the Second World War, and in the 1950s was able to set up a forge in a rural setting at Hampton Lovett, near Droitwich in Worcestershire. Much of his work was ecclesiastical – designing and making church furnishings and undertaking restoration works to gates including at Tewkesbury Abbey and the cathedrals at Gloucester,

Worcester, Sheffield, Manchester and Truro. He received numerous commissions for St Michael's Church at Baddesley Clinton in Warwickshire. Of particular interest to contemporary sensibilities is an altar cross and candlesticks made for the church in 1968 to a simple but powerful design, re-using ironwork from the east window that had been replaced with bronze.

In 1974, Alan Evans (who had trained as an art teacher at Shoreditch College of Education and started out making silver jewellery), was offered workshop space in return for help with heavy work in Knight's forge at Hampton Lovett. It was not the easiest of relationships; Evans was a young man brimming with new ideas, while Knight was a traditionalist and somewhat set in his ways. It was an interesting set-up though – a craft community with the potter Geoffrey Whiting's workshop next door. (Whiting's son David, also a potter, became a close friend of Alan's.) It certainly provided Alan with the opportunity to develop his skills and experience with forged metal. He assisted Knight on big commissions, including the restoration of the Davies brothers' gates at Erddig Park in the mid-1970s for the National Trust, a project Alan described as his main blacksmith training and a bit of an eye-opener. Thinking about it later, he described the significance to himself, 'a strapping 23-year-old' as he put it, working with Knight, 'the then (as I perceived him) old man of 60', of working slowly with deliberate actions. In a subsequent online post (Alan Evans iforgeiron.com, 22 September 2012), he described their working process to a fellow blacksmith as a perfect example of learning by doing:

> 'We were working heat for heat on rolled snub scrolls and water leaves in wrought iron. First thing after I had lit the fire, he would take a bar, heat it, work it. I would have my piece in the fire beside his and as soon as he'd finish I'd try and reproduce exactly what he'd done, brilliant training! Trouble was after a few heats my piece was lagging and I was trying to copy what he had done two heats before! By the time we got to coffee break I had to work through with another 5 heats to catch up. I was absolutely knackered and running with sweat from the strength, energy and speed of movement, he… never broke a sweat or seemed to hurry!'

The Cotswolds Arts and Crafts movement provided Alan with a tough and demanding model against which to measure himself. He was conscious of the high quality of work achieved by Gimson, Bucknell and others and aware that he was seen by some as following in their footsteps. There were very obvious occasions such as when, in about 2000, he was commissioned to make a number of brass candle sconces to sit alongside others made by Bucknell to Gimson's design in the living room of a private house in the south Cotswolds. They are still there today – not reproductions, but rather Alan's contemporary take on the originals, using the simple daffodils that proliferate in the spring as his inspiration. They have a confidence and strong character of their own.

Photo Katannuta Brown

The Millennium Beacon, made by Alan Evans for the Centenary of the Whiteway Colony, 1998, now sited on the spot where the title deeds were ceremonially burned

ASHBEE AND GIMSON

C. R. Ashbee (1863–1942) and Ernest W. Gimson (1864–1919) were leading members of the Arts and Crafts movement. They both trained as architects, but made their greatest impact as designer/makers. They believed in the importance of creative manual work for the individual and for the good of society.

Ashbee's Guild of Handicraft took shape in London's East End. He trained and employed young local men without any previous experience to make furniture, metalwork, jewellery and leatherwork. He also set up a smithy making fire tools, candlesticks and so on. His fine metalwork designs were mainly in silver with repoussé decoration (a metalworking technique in which a malleable metal is shaped by hammering from the reverse side to create a design in low relief), and delicate wirework. He moved the Guild to Chipping Campden, Gloucestershire in 1902, convinced that a country setting would benefit his craftsmen.

Gimson had already made the move from London to the south Cotswolds. He settled near the village of Sapperton in 1893 making turned ladderback chairs and decorative plasterwork before renting a workshop and employing craftsmen to make his furniture designs. In about 1902 he also set up a smithy employing first Alfred Bucknell, a young local smith, and then a few others to make objects such as gates, door furniture, sconces and firedogs. Norman Bucknell, Alfred's son, continued to make pieces to Gimson's design in his forge at Bisley until his death in 2006.

Gimson design for a candle sconce, 1905–15

TRADITIONAL BLACKSMITHING – THE PENWITH GATE

So much of our landscape, our towns, our public buildings and our homes are touched by the work of the blacksmith. Once the centre of the community, the blacksmith was the shoe-er of horses, the mender of machinery, the nail-maker and creator of swords, shovels, knives, forks, pots, ploughs and ritual objects in many cultures. Yet we take the iron all around us – the handrail, boot scraper, latch, lock, knocker, candlestick holder, worked by unknown families of smiths – for granted. We handle and use this iron; its understated modesty is testimony to its workability. Undemanding and unsigned, we overlook it – until we trip over the old gate as it quietly rusts away in a hedge.

Such is the story of the Penwith gate. It is deeply local – only found in the Penwith peninsula, west Cornwall. The age and origins of its design and construction are unknown; certainly earlier than the only known photograph from the 1880s it happens to be in. It is efficient, elegant and clever, designed and constructed before the invention of welding, so put together with traditional screw threads and nuts. It took Peter Parkinson, another blacksmith from another age, to unearth this gate, bring it out of the shadows, and celebrate the work of an unknown smith. His idea that this gate might have been transported over rough terrain as a bundle of bars and assembled on site, with a handful of square nuts, is testimony to the problem-solving inventiveness of the blacksmith that blacksmiths in all ages inherit.

This piece owes everything to the research passion of Peter Parkinson

An example of a Penwith gate, west Cornwall

EARTH FIRE IRON

ARTIST PROFILE

CHRISTOPH FRIEDRICH

As a passionate blacksmith, I succumbed to the allure of iron more than 50 years ago. I am fascinated by the craftsmanship of the process; by the possibility of finding shapes with – and in – iron using the natural elements of fire, water and air.

During my basic training as a craftsman, I got to know different design approaches and subsequently went on to use them to form my own. Following my conviction that good design requires good craftsmanship, I place emphasis on execution right from the design phase. In my work, I always try to reflect the time in which I live. I want to learn from the experiences of the past in order to create something new. I get clues and inspiration by going through the world with open eyes, observing nature and valuing simplicity and honesty. Sometimes a poem emerges from my design thoughts. Nature in particular often offers me clues for a line, for a form. Exactly copying nature or repeating designed works from the past was never an issue for me.

A huge amount of effort has already gone into transforming the basic material that a blacksmith works with before it can be processed further in the workshop. I believe – as Alan did – that this prior effort should be visible in our work and that the forging technique should only be used where the shape requires it. Clear, simple forms where nothing is unnecessary make comprehensibility possible.

I consider it a privilege that my wife, Margrit, and I were able to buy and renovate a unique, water-powered hammer forge in Switzerland 45 years ago. This magical place, with its archaic furnishings, influenced my thinking and my design, as well as instilling a life-long sense of awe for simplicity. It is – and has always been – important to me to be able to share, pass on and preserve this conviction. This way of thinking has led to many beautiful connections, encounters and friendships, including with Alan, who I first met in 1980 at a British Artist Blacksmith's event in Hereford. Our common way of thinking was always visible in our designs, something which sparked inner satisfaction and preserved our friendship.

Christoph Friedrich Sculpture 'Dependence on each Other', Private Collection

Christoph Friedrich forging in his water-hammer-driven forge

ALAN EVANS AND THE NEW IRON AGE

Peter Parkinson

Peter Parkinson studied at the Royal College of Art and worked as a designer in London Transport's Architects' Department and at Allied Ironfounders. He lectured at Farnham for 25 years while learning blacksmithing at Richard Quinnell's large forge at Dorking. In 1992 he set up his own business in Hampshire, designing and making forged architectural metalwork and public art. He has written widely on blacksmithing and sculptural metalwork. He closed his large workshop in 2015 and moved to West Penwith in Cornwall where he has a small forging workshop.

Alan was a dear and inspirational friend who I knew and valued for more than 40 years. Alan and blacksmithing have been inextricably linked in my mind since I came across blacksmithing as an art college senior lecturer and was invited to the Crafts Council's Forging Iron conference and workshops at Hereford College of Arts in 1979 and 1980. I gained work experience at Richard Quinnell's extensive forge and was immediately hooked. A year or two later, I was able to set up and teach what became a BA (Hons) Metals course at West Surrey College of Art and Design (now the University College of Creative Arts in Farnham, Surrey). Regrettably since writing this, I discover the course has now ceased.

Chestnut Roaster designed and made by Alan Evans, purchased by Richard Quinnell 1983/4

In 1982, long after the crafts of ceramics, textiles, jewellery, furniture and hot glass had been firmly established as creative activities in Farnham, blacksmithing became an art college subject. I was able to equip the college with four forges that were due to be scrapped from a school in Guildford, despite being concerned that I was assisting the termination of blacksmithing at the school. Since my blacksmithing experience was limited – I was only a little ahead of the students – it was a steep learning curve. I had to work hard: analysing techniques, reading texts, developing hand skills and constructing my own home forge. Through the British Artist Blacksmiths Association (BABA), I met numbers of blacksmiths – including Alan – and learned from them all. Later, I was able to invite a few blacksmiths to visit the college, to demonstrate and talk to the students. As an outsider, I was able to look at the blacksmith's craft from a creative point of view and consider its aims and objectives. What did it stand for? Where was it going? In many ways, I looked to Alan for answers, not verbal perhaps, but seeing how he worked. Two or three BABA conferences were held at the college. A decade later, I resigned my college post to set up my own blacksmithing business.

So what do blacksmiths do? For a start they don't shoe horses, that is the specialist province of the farrier. A 'smith' is a metalworker – hence goldsmith, silversmith and coppersmith – while the 'black' in blacksmith refers to the dark grey oxide that forms on hot iron or steel.

Forging

All blacksmiths shape hot metal with a hand and/or power hammer, working at an anvil – an action known as 'forging'. But what they make by forging varies widely. Typically, pieces range from small items such as coat hooks, candleholders and paperknives to large architectural elements including stair balustrades, gates and one-off pieces to commission, but the possibilities are endless. If, as we are told, a mine is a hole in the ground with a Cornishman in it, then a forge is a building containing something you are likely never to have seen before.

Photo © Chris Fairclough

Detail of a public art project by Alan Evans and Sue Ridge at the railway station, Southampton, since removed

The terminology of metalworking is often inexact and confusing. How, for example, did the good honest word 'forging' become a synonym for 'faking'? The 'forge' is both the blacksmith's fire and the blacksmith's workplace. 'Wrought' is the archaic word for 'worked'. Wrought iron is low carbon, historic iron. Confusion arises here in using the name of a metal to describe a decorative piece of metalwork as 'wrought ironwork' when it may in fact be steel.

Steel is defined as an alloy of iron and carbon. Mild steel contains a fractional percentage of carbon and is the metal most often used by blacksmiths. Steel with a little more carbon is harder and is used to make tools, but when the carbon content reaches three or four percent, paradoxically the metal is called cast iron rather than steel. Wrought iron is an almost chemically pure form of iron, physically mixed with silica slag, a historic material no longer produced but available as a re-rolled salvaged product.

The term 'artist blacksmith' is used to distinguish our activities from those of industrial blacksmiths who make tools and engineering components. Industrial blacksmiths were employed by NASA to forge special alloys in the demanding days of the race to get men to the moon in the 1960s.

In design terms, traditional blacksmithing features a range of historic motifs such as scrolls of particular kinds, leaves and twists, in a visual distillation of eighteenth- and nineteenth-century ironwork; a vocabulary of distinct forms, frozen in time, which were seen as comprising the structure of blacksmithing. The fundamental forging processes – moving hot metal with hammer and anvil, tapering, bending, twisting, spreading, upsetting, punching holes or welding in the fire – are common to both traditional and contemporary blacksmiths, so perhaps the traditional blacksmiths saw these motifs as the expression of a heritage; a way of keeping alive 'real' blacksmithing skills with their own ethics and practice. These, for example, ruled out electric arc welding, developed in the First World War, in favour of 'more authentic' fire-welding.

In a way, this view is entirely understandable. After the First World War, the Government had set up the Rural Industries Bureau to support small businesses in the countryside. Between 1952 and 1962, the Bureau published a series of small instructive books – chapters in a blacksmith's bible – neatly detailing basic blacksmithing processes. These remained in print into the twenty-first century and have informed generations of blacksmiths.

In 1968 the Rural Industries Bureau was merged into a new body – the Council for Small Industries in Rural Areas (CoSIRA). Its role was to support and make rural businesses more viable, an objective expressed as 'advice, backed by technical and management services'. In 1973 it published a *Catalogue of Drawings for Wrought Iron*. This was essentially a pattern book of designs, which blacksmiths could show to their clients. Once the client had chosen a particular design, the blacksmith would send the dimensions to CoSIRA who would then supply layout drawings for the blacksmith to work from. This quite remarkable help and service was created with the best of intentions but, sadly its effect was regressive, since it relegated blacksmiths to being little more than makers with no creative input of their own. Don't think – just make. This catalogue remained in print for many years and is still available online.

BABA was initiated in 1979 by Jinny and Richard Quinnell and has published a journal, now called *Artist Blacksmith*, continuously recording metalwork, people and events since July 1979. (When in the future art historians come to write a history of blacksmithing in Britain, this magazine will be invaluable in providing the data.) BABA brought blacksmiths scattered across the country in touch with each other, often for the first time. Many, I have been told, thought that in 1979 they were the last real blacksmith in Britain. These were exciting days for a craft, but this new association had its problems. Through some of the early years, there was a degree of suspicion between the older traditionally trained blacksmiths and newcomers like me, and I suspect Alan, who had originally trained to be a craft teacher, started a career making jewellery, then began working part time for traditional blacksmith Alan Knight. He was captivated by the forging processes and set up his own forge workshop. He commented that 'blacksmithing just meant a bigger hammer', but he also believed that it was his art. It is intriguing that the creative and eminent American blacksmith and sculptor, Albert Paley (born 1944), was also originally a jeweller.

So at the same time as BABA was bring blacksmiths together, the 'traditional' members had every reason to be concerned that their values were under threat. They may not all have used the CoSIRA opportunities but clearly some felt that what blacksmiths did was being questioned. There was talk of arc welders – an anathema to the traditional craftsman – lurking out of sight, under a sack in the forge, and the idea that blacksmiths might ignore traditional motifs altogether seemed for a time to be a kind of heresy.

Excerpt from *A new booke of drawings invented and designed by Jean Tijou*, 1693.

Despite the inventiveness of medieval blacksmiths and the creativity exemplified by the influential Jean Tijou and later British smiths such as Robert Blackwell, William Edney and the Roberts Brothers in the 1700s, it seemed that in 1980 individual creativity was almost a new concept for blacksmiths in Britain. Things were different on the continent where blacksmithing design had moved on as a contemporary craft, absorbing the fashions of the time. Art Nouveau and Art Deco had provided remarkable creative inspiration for continental blacksmiths who responded to each movement in the same way as fine artists, other craftspeople and architects. While somehow in England blacksmiths and architects – with the notable exception of Charles Rennie Mackintosh – had essentially missed out on the opportunity.

In the early 1980s, in the early days of BABA, artist blacksmiths looked across the channel and saw amazing things in France, Germany, Belgium, Italy and further afield too. Blacksmiths there clearly reflected their times with joy and enthusiasm, in designs without a trace of 'traditional' decorative detail. They had moved on, and sometimes created work using complex and interesting construction details – joints in effect – as decoration. So rather than a structure with applied decoration, the structure itself provided the aesthetic. This was creativity and imagination of a different kind; bold, confident and intriguing – its own kind of blacksmithing, exemplified in the work of blacksmiths such as Achim Kühn, Herman Gradinger and Paul Zimmermann.

Photo courtesy of Lesley Greene

Alan Evans forging one of six trophies for the Royal Society of Arts, 1987

Early on people from very different backgrounds joined BABA, all of them enthusiastic, eager to learn and unconstrained by traditional values. They were just trying things out. These were exciting times. Alan was at the forefront of that movement. I think, in his view (and mine), it wasn't a question of using the right or wrong tools, it was a question of what you did with them – the output. He had no inhibitions about arc welding, for example, which could be neat and visible, or entirely unseen. He bought a power hammer very early on too, using it with remarkable control, to forge light and elegant chestnut roasters of ladle form and even stainless steel teaspoons. Just a little time later, he was using that same power hammer to make his large, wonderful gates for the Treasury in the Crypt of St Paul's Cathedral. They were a revelation for British blacksmithing. *(See p56)*

Alan epitomised that exciting, creative period, when we all waited eagerly to see the next piece of work from a few remarkably innovative, leading blacksmiths. Not celebrities living distant lives, but people we could meet and talk to, who were happy to answer questions, explain and inform. The exchange of ideas was remarkable. Nobody said no; if you asked how or why they did something, they would tell you.

Even among this group of stellar blacksmiths, Alan stood out, quietly demonstrating his creative vision, avoiding stereotypes and very much ploughing his own creative furrow. I don't think he saw his approach to blacksmithing as reacting to, or against anything, it was always a matter of solving a problem and exploring what could be done with hot metal with the same spirit as those seventeenth-century smiths who had innovated and pushed at the boundaries with the vision and tools of their age.

A notable and delightful example of Alan's experimental approach was the elegant steel handrail at one side of the straight flight of stairs in his own home. It was octagonal in section, delicately tapered towards each end from a heavy central mounting where it looped briefly, to be trapped between the only fixing – three large, round pins. He also spent time early on experimenting with rolled steel sections and large steel tubes, not normally considered by blacksmiths. He made a number of intriguing sculptural pieces, cutting into them, bending out sections and forging them. He also revisited the traditional blacksmithing process of twisting metal, using the technique not only on straight bars, but also – memorably - on one with a right-angled corner. He similarly forged a deep notch in heavy steel plate and twisted that as part of the structure of a gate.

Staircase Handrail 1986, private collection

Alan could draw well by hand, but he engaged with new technology, designing work and developing complex drawings on a computer screen, using up-to-the-minute software. He shared this skill with us too, demonstrating it all and discussing computer drafting with such enthusiasm and evident effect that many of us bought our first computer. (I never did use mine to draw.) Similarly, because his work became so large, he frequently used a power hammer or hydraulic press – high-tech tools that seemed wonderfully unlikely in his rural Gloucestershire workshop. This was a place, after all, where the Arts and Crafts movement was alive and well.

Alan wasn't intimidated by scale. His work was often huge, requiring a crane to support the workpiece under the power hammer or hydraulic press. But this never overwhelmed a sensitivity to the site, and the work retained a human touch. There is an environmental effect that Alan well understood. Make something that looks very large in the workshop, then take it to its intended site outdoors and – sometimes alarmingly – it seems to shrink. He understood scale – his cross on the Ecumenical Church, Milton Keynes is physically massive, but is perfectly proportioned, high on the dome of the building.

He was an original and brilliant designer, and the computer was his drawing board. He saw design as a series of problems to solve and he knew how to identify and define those problems and also how to relate work to each specific site. 'Site-specific art' is a familiar term, but identifying the aspect to focus on demands considerable research, thought and imagination. The St Paul's Treasury gates embodied visual echoes of the curved vaulting of the crypt ceiling stonework and reflected Christian imagery in a trinity of curving crosses.

Alan responded creatively to practical problems too. For example, in his work for pedestrian schemes in both Cheltenham and the London borough of Lewisham, he designed cycle racks which exploited the strength of cantilevered stainless-steel loops set into heavy punched bars, which only needed four ground fixings – far simpler and more elegant to install than a commercially available system with 18 ground fixings.

Iron and steel are commonplace, but they are also special materials. Cheap by metal standards and particularly poor conductors of heat, they allow the blacksmith to, for example, isolate a yellow-hot portion, making it soft enough to precisely locate a bend, or allow the smith to hold the cold end of a short bar in a bare hand while the other end is hot forged. There is something magical in using the simplest and crudest of tools – a hammer – to control and transform an unprepossessing piece of steel bar into a precise, useful, meaningful – even delicate – form, shaping it plastically like a piece of modelling clay.

The physical skill of blacksmiths is remarkable (and you get to play with fire!), but it is seldom seen or appreciated by the public. The days when children huddled round the door of the old village forge watching the blacksmith are long gone. Some skills are hard to explain and can only be attributed to the proverbial 10,000 hours of practice. In a blacksmithing class, somebody will invariably ask, 'How can you be sure that the hammer will hit the hot metal at a precise place?' The answer is, 'I can't explain it'. Clearly, if the hammer is swung from above head height, by the time it is visible, it is too late to aim it towards a precise point. But a blacksmith can hit that point every time, even with a variety of different-sized hammers, and at different angles. These are learned skills and they are impressive.

Power hammers require just as much skill. They will strike the same place on the anvil every time. The smith has a foot pedal to control the impact, but still must manoeuvre the workpiece under the hammer so that it hits the right place every time. It is important to appreciate that the hot bar gets a little longer, or wider, or both with every hit. It is possible to correct errors on a small bar held in one hand, but imagine manoeuvring a massive bar, maybe 100mm square, supported by a crane hoist. Such things were a day's work for Alan and the blacksmiths and apprentices he worked with. So many of Alan's pieces are huge. Huge might imply lumpy, but Alan's work was never that; it was always beautifully formed and beautifully judged.

It has to be said that Alan's ambition for a kind of perfection – which wasn't always what the client was asking for – could cause problems. This wasn't the attitude of a self-opinionated, arrogant man, but rather a sincere, considered and reasoned search for the best answer; even if it cost him time and money. Several of Alan's commissions were won in design competitions involving other blacksmiths or sculptors, although – characteristically – he always said that design shouldn't be a competitive activity, since the real competition was with himself – to produce the best design he could.

In the entrance to the towering City of London development at Broadgate, his long screen – made in response to a commission to make something to deter vehicles from entering the large paved area – is a massive work in metal. It is perfect in the context of the angular modern high-rise buildings, providing a dancing, rippling, humanising effect down at ground level.

Photo courtesy of Lesley Greene

'Go Between' 1990–91, screen by Alan Evans, commissioned by Rosehaugh Stanhope Broadgate Development, City of London. Currently in storage pending re-location

ALAN EVANS AND THE NEW IRON AGE

There are so many examples of Alan's work that could be discussed, but his work at the Public Record Office at Kew, London is, in my opinion, his finest. It is stunning in concept, brilliant in execution and remarkable in that the design was commissioned by the government – not a body known for its adventurous aesthetic taste. The Record Office entrance, approached along a traditional street of residential Victorian villas, is marked by towering forged structures emerging from the boundary fence, which is also forged. It brings to mind the masts and spars of square-rigged ships and is an intriguing juxtaposition with the streetscape. The construction is based on tally sticks, a simple medieval system of cuts and notches in short hazel sticks, used to record tax payments in an early method of record-keeping. It is a satisfying visual reference to the building's purpose. Beyond the gate on the approach to the building are additional powerful and interesting balustrades leading over the bridge to the front door. In my view, it is a remarkable memorial for a remarkable man.

Photo courtesy of Lesley Greene

Two details from Alan Evans' major project of entrance gates and railings at the Public Record Office, Kew, 1992

CHARLES RENNIE MACKINTOSH
(1868–1928)

The Scottish architect's Glasgow School of Art (1899–c. 1908) is acknowledged as an internationally significant work of art and architecture in which the integration of ironwork is an essential part of the building's design, fabric and decoration. Much of the ironwork was massive, simple and functional and was made by local blacksmiths. 'T' girders support the main roof timbers and, according to Jefferson Barnes in his book, *Charles Rennie Mackintosh. Ironwork and Metalwork at Glasgow School of Art,* Glasgow School of Art, Glasgow, 1978, their split and forged forms were so complex that they caused a strike amongst the blacksmiths forging them. These are not traditional scrolls. The 26 great window brackets are long, straight bars that end with multiple clusters; these give rigidity to the architecture but also serve as platforms for the window cleaners' planks. The surrounding railings are tall straight rails with central clusters of simple 'stamens' – indicative of Mackintosh's interest in botanical forms. To have seen this building and its ironwork before the great fire in 2014, and a second fire in 2018, was to have been present before an iconic work of art.

Detail of the window brackets at Glasgow School of Art designed by C.R. Mackintosh, c. 1900

Photo courtesy of The Glasgow School of Art

PIONEERING BRITISH BLACKSMITHS

The Victoria and Albert Museum's exhibition, 'Towards a New Iron Age' in 1982 hailed the renaissance in British blacksmithing and established artist blacksmiths as an exciting force in the United Kingdom's arts and crafts culture. While many British blacksmiths of that period (Antony Robinson, Alan Dawson, Ian Lamb, John Creed, Brian Russell and others) made a significant contribution to this new aesthetic, those profiled here are particularly relevant to this publication.

The catalogue accompanying the 1982 V&A exhibition

RICHARD QUINNELL

Quinnell has a played a critical role in the emergence of artist blacksmithing. His traditional family business was successful, but by the early 1970s, he was quoted in Amina Chatwin's *Into the New Iron Age: Modern British Blacksmiths* (Coach House Publishing, 1995) saying, '[I] …honestly thought we were the last firm of blacksmiths in the world'. Encouraged by the then Crafts Advisory Committee (later the Crafts Council), Quinnell won a Churchill Travelling Scholarship to explore European blacksmithing. He met smiths such as the Kühn family and Herman Gradinger who were making contemporary sculpture, creating new forms from traditional techniques, and were valued for their work in public places. With the support of his wife, Jinny, he set up the British Artist Blacksmiths Association (BABA) which, by championing young smiths, arranging forge-ins and blacksmithing events and bringing foreign smiths to meet and share ideas, is the best (and least hierarchical) resource for blacksmiths in the United Kingdom. He and Jinny opened the Fire and Iron gallery in Leatherhead in 1982 and, in addition, hosted space at the forge for younger smiths where they could make larger works for public places. Richard Quinnell is still a seminal personality, much respected in international artist blacksmithing.

'For Max – Lament for a Lost Generation' Richard Quinnell 2016. Made for the Transition exhibition, Ypres, and then in Hereford Cathedral. Hot forged fabricated aluminium and steel with forge clinker, resin and paint

PETER PARKINSON

Parkinson was lecturer in metalwork at West Surrey College of Art and Design (now the University College of Art and Design Farnham) from 1972–1992. Renowned as a highly knowledgeable and inspirational teacher and writer, as well as a practitioner, his teaching policy included a strong programme of visiting lecturers (including Alan Evans) and demonstrators to inspire the students. He ensured that Farnham hosted two seminal BABA conferences, which were attended by British sculptors and featured demonstrations by international artist blacksmiths. Parkinson's personal work is refined and elegant, often domestic in scale such as bowls, clocks and mirrors. He was one of the titular *Six British Blacksmiths* in the touring exhibition organised by the British Crafts Centre in the Minories gallery, Colchester in 1983. His larger public artworks include the 'Dorking Cockerel' in 2007, which is now a popular landmark.

Peter Parkinson in his studio with the 'Dorking Cockerel' commissioned from Fire and Iron Ltd by David Maltby as Chair of Mole Valley District Council, 2007

PIONEERING BRITISH BLACKSMITHS

STUART HILL

Hill was arguably one of the most inventive designer blacksmiths of the 'new iron age'. Although he made little himself – commissioning others to make the work – he was the first artist blacksmith to have a one-man show in the Britain (at the Minories gallery in Colchester in 1981). He challenged traditional forging techniques, including forging tiny frogs from a one-inch square bar. Inspired by the movements of water, he designed gates, fences and grilles with rippling and reflective forms, which later morphed into moiré patterns that created optical illusions. He was constantly exploring good design and was inspired by other forms, such as origami or pull-out Christmas decorations. He invented the seven-petalled seat, prototyped by the Quinnell Workshop, from one piece of tubing; seven seats created by cutting up a tube and opening it out. The cleverness, relative cheapness and efficiency of his approach meant he could go into production, founding Claydon Architectural Metalwork. He drew on Computer Aided Design (CAD) systems that meant his ideas could be shared – and perhaps exploited by others whose works were not always of such a high quality. Hill was also the first editor of *British Artist Blacksmith* magazine, and the seven editions he oversaw set quality standards for future editions.

Photo from 'Metalworks' 1999, Klaus Pracht

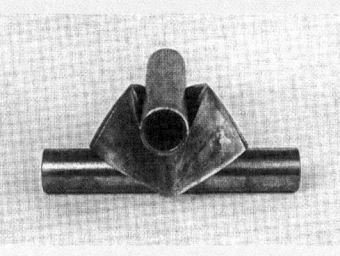

'The Claydon Clamp', 1982 by Stuart Hill. Hot-formed, sliced square steel tube between two round tubes

JIM HORROBIN

Horrobin is a key figure in British blacksmithing. The son of an armourer who espoused the Peace Movement and became a blacksmith, Horrobin worked in his father's forge in Somerset. Traditionally trained, he was widely known as an exceptional traditional craftsman and won prizes for decorative pieces at local agricultural shows. By the mid-1970s, he had begun to experiment – especially with natural forms – and became a founder member of BABA. An unusually 'open' commission for a gate to a vegetable garden allowed him the freedom to use experimental hand forging and (for the period) innovative forms inspired by the landscape. He won the 1982 Victoria and Albert Museum's selected competition for its metalwork gallery. This was followed by a number of prestigious commissions, including the Winston Churchill Memorial Gates at St Paul's Cathedral, London, in 2005.

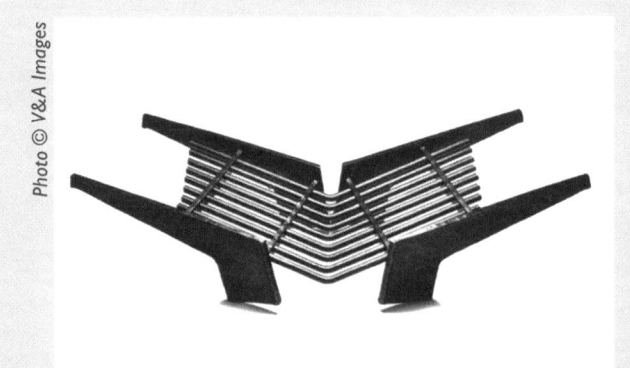

Photo © V&A Images

Fire basket in mild steel by Jim Horrobin, 1980

ST PAUL'S CATHEDRAL GATES

Sandy Nairne

Lift up your heads, O ye gates; and be ye lift up, ye everlasting doors…
Psalm 24:7, The Messiah, part 33

In the Crypt at St Paul's are a pair of very striking gates running floor to ceiling at the entrance to the Treasury, facing to the north, designed and made by Alan Evans more than 40 years ago and now regarded as a masterwork.

The design of the new Treasury area of the Crypt was undertaken by the London consultants, Higgins Ney Design Unit. New patronage of the arts by the church had been in discussion and at the suggestion of Phillipa Glanville, then senior curator of silver and metalwork at the Victoria and Albert Museum, the Cathedral decided to commission new gates. Alan was then selected from five artist blacksmiths shortlisted by the Crafts Council in 1980. The contract was confirmed in March 1981, and just over three months later, on 26 June, the gates were delivered.

Forged and rivetted, each leaf pivots on an axis between the stone floor and the ceiling, and all the braces and struts (both major and minor) have wonderfully faceted surfaces: each hammer blow legible without interrupting the strength and clarity of the whole. The curves within the gates, swooping parabola-like, echo the vaults of the space behind, while intricate metal locks and bolts ensure their purpose is explicit as guardians of the Cathedral's most precious objects.

Some years after the inauguration of the Treasury Gates, the Cathedral decided to change the use of the space to create an immersive environment of projected images, entitled Oculus, and designed to give those with physical impairments a version of exploring the Whispering Gallery, Dome and the Lantern. It is currently used as a space for exhibitions related to the Cathedral, but the gates remain.

Writing soon after the gates were unveiled, blacksmithing expert Amina Chatwin, commented on how Alan had 'produced a brilliantly conceived strong barrier, with all the natural grace of a web hung across a cave mouth'. And that concept of the magical nature of spiders' webs was celebrated in a recent haiku by poet laureate Simon Armitage. Written for the Lost Gardens of Heligan in Cornwall and entitled *Web*, Armitage described how 'Abseiling silk threads, spiders darn holes in the hedge'. In that spirit, Alan took one element from the natural world and translated it through fire into Wren's perfectly proportioned architecture.

The American artist Carl Andre referred to his sculptures as a 'cut in space' and in that sense Alan Evans' gates are poised between a division of spaces (allowing no visitors inside when closed and locked) and an invitation to be curious: to lean forward and peer in. There is a delightful delicacy to the work, both in proportion and construction, an aspect of Alan's work emphasised by Lisa Wood in her February 2023 obituary for the *Guardian* in which she reported how at a conference of blacksmiths in 1992 he said that 'the difference between making jewellery and ironwork was simply picking up a heavier hammer, but he thought of jewellery as his craft and blacksmithing as his art'.

Photo © Angelo Hornak

Treasury Gates St Paul's Cathedral, Alan Evans, 1981

EARTH FIRE IRON

Alan Evans working on the St Paul's Gates

METAL AT ST PAUL'S CATHEDRAL

For a massive stone building, St Paul's Cathedral has a surprising number of important metal elements. Some iron work goes back to its construction, including famously, when Christopher Wren inserted a great iron chain (cased in lead) into the stone at the base of the dome to contain the side thrust from the inner brick cone that supports the weight of the Lantern. He also commissioned the brilliant Huguenot blacksmith, Jean Tijou, to design and fashion the screens and grilles around the Quire and balustrades for the Whispering Gallery.

More controversially, a set of large-scale cast iron railings were added around St Paul's as the Cathedral was being completed, against Wren's wishes, who was no longer surveyor. The Victoria and Albert Museum has a section of these railings in its collection. The Collections catalogue describes them as, 'the earliest of English cast iron railings, cast by Richard Jones Smith between 1710 and 1714'. All 200 tons were hauled to the Cathedral from his Lamberhurst Foundry in Sussex.

Later, great bells were cast in bronze and added to the Western towers, including Great Paul, the largest bell in Britain in current use, which was cast by John Taylor and Co. in 1881 and weighs 16.75 imperial tons (17.02 metric tonnes).

RENEWAL AT ST PAUL'S

Today, near the boundary railings, we find much lighter gauge rails above the new ramps on each side of the North Transept, conceived by Martin Stancliffe and designed by Oliver Caroe, present surveyor to the fabric. They were completed in 2022 and include aluminium bronze uprights manufactured in Italy with discrete LED lights set into the handrails. Beautifully proportioned and spaced, the whole arrangement is a crucial addition to the Cathedral.

At the start of the new millennium, St Paul's had commissioned a 1.6m high hanging pyx from the silversmith Rod Kelly, who fashioned an exquisite silver container for the consecrated bread of the Eucharist with chased and embossed patterning. The commission was skillfully guided by Peter Burman, my predecessor as chair of the Fabric Advisory Committee. And in 2004, the Cathedral commissioned the massive Winston Churchill Memorial Gates by Jim Horrobin at the entrance to the memorial section of the Crypt. Weighing three tonnes, Horrobin forged his gates from steel, bronze and naval brass. More malleable than ordinary brass, this allowed him to make an internal shift in the design: turning the tips of the bayonets on the depicted muskets into the blades of harrows and hoes.

The Churchill Gates sit in appropriate counterpoint to the Treasury Gates, with more narrative and symbolism than Alan Evans' earlier and more abstract work. Both Horrobin and Alan grew up within traditional craft families with workshops and both became central to the artist blacksmith resurgence of the 1980s and 1990s. The convergence of their work in the Crypt at St Paul's stands as testimony to their innovative contributions to the hugely important renewal of the fine art of blacksmithing.

I am grateful to Lesley Greene for spending time with me at St Paul's Cathedral and offering her insights into Alan's work, and to Mary Greensted for her perceptive comments and for drawing my attention to the article by Alan Evans about the St Paul's Gates in Crafts *54, January/February 1982.*

Alan Evans working on the St Paul's Gates

ARTIST PROFILE

SAM PEARCE

Iron and coal run in my blood. My mother's grandfather drove a hammer in the steel mills of Sheffield, while my dad's grandfather spent most of his working life down the coal mines in County Durham.

I'm still unsure what exactly triggered my curiosity of the blacksmith's craft and, at the age of 16, I was unaware of quite how entangled in forged metal my life would become. However, I told my dad I would like to be a blacksmith and his first thoughts were that we better go and meet one.

Our closest forge was Brian Russell's and, after a brief telephone conversation, he invited us to visit him in Little Newsham, Darlington. Brian showed us around the workshop and, as we passed the diesel furnace, he shoved a piece of bar in front of me to forge under the Pilkington power hammer. He showed me how to operate the hammer using the foot treadle and then let me set about this piece of round bar with great gusto. That very brief – but captivating – encounter must have sparked something in me; I was hooked.

Initially, design wasn't much of a consideration in the work I was producing; I would just copy small projects from books. Then I was introduced to Peat Oberon and The School of Blacksmithing, a purpose-built teaching facility based at Preston Hall Museum near Stockton-on-Tees, who fostered my enthusiasm and introduced me to traditional blacksmithing. I was still at school and I didn't have a long-term plan, great ambition or goal; I kept picking up a hammer simply for the pleasure of working with hot steel. I enjoyed the difficulty of forging, the all-consuming process of a physical and mental challenge. My only aspiration was to just keep forging.

It was Peat who suggested I applied to the artist blacksmithing degree at Hereford College of Arts. I lived and breathed forged metal during my time there, spending most of my time experimenting with different forms and techniques and then trying to squeeze them into a project. My work at this point was busy and crowded with different textures and forms. Although I was enjoying the process of making this work, the completed piece often lacked clarity and it became apparent that the more I added during the making, the more I took away from the final outcome. This realisation led my practice in a completely different direction. It was during this time that I came across Alan and I found his ethos motivated me to keep exploring new ideas.

Photo © Mat Dixon

Sam Pearce

I was incredibly fortunate to engage in email conversations with Alan in which we discussed the philosophy behind his work. In one he wrote, 'But we owe ourselves the freedom as artists to beware of making rules for ourselves… we want to explore opportunities and not impose self-imposed restrictions.' I thought this was such a balanced view and it was liberating to hear at a time when I was so focused on one direction. He also explained the virtues of a tapered octagonal handrail, pointing out that the forged octagon provides a tactile interaction, as well as having functional attributes, because it acts as a brake as your grip gets tighter as you go down and pull yourself up. This is such a beautifully simple idea and still reminds me to consider each detail.

Photo courtesy of the artist

'Link Bench', forged mild steel with ash, by Sam Pearce, 2013

When I left college, I found myself working for a relatively large blacksmithing firm in the north of England that specialised in restoration and large-scale projects. I was lucky enough to work alongside some knowledgeable blacksmiths, honing my skills on prestigious projects. During this time my own practice was set to one side. However, the hours spent working on and studying traditional ironwork were not wasted, providing me with a vast array of forged solutions that I can call upon in my own projects today.

Heritage ironwork is full of functional forged details that were made out of necessity rather than luxury. Fire, hammer and anvil were the technology of the day, and those blacksmiths came up with all sorts of elegant ways to solve problems.

Now I choose to make work in the way haiku is written. I try to be concise yet descriptive with the forgings that are used. My work aims to capture the immediacy of the forging process that first drew me to practise as a blacksmith. I aspire to work with a lightness of touch in order to demonstrate the plasticity of steel known only by the blacksmith. With this I like to challenge myself to create work that appears simple in design but is intricate and complex in the structure and build. For me, each piece of work is an opportunity to confront those design questions and continue to explore and challenge myself.

Photo courtesy of the artist

'Wave Gate', forged mild steel, by Sam Pearce, 2019

ALAN EVANS: EARTH, MATERIAL, PRACTICE

Paul Harper

Paul Harper has recently retired as a lecturer in Visual Cultures at Middlesex University and London Metropolitan University. His research interests have been focused on craft-making and craftspeople. He is a board member of the Crafts Study Centre, a research centre, archive and collection of modern British crafts.

Alan Evans was born and raised at Whiteway, a community near Stroud, in the Cotswolds, founded in the late nineteenth century along Tolstoyan, agrarian and anarchist principles. Alan's grandparents were among the members who settled there in the 1920s. His parents were Quakers and craftspeople – his father was a furniture maker, his mother a woodcarver – and Alan was raised in an atmosphere of creativity, ideology and respect for the environment. As an adult, his workshop was adjacent to his childhood home. He lived nearby with his partner, Lesley, where they built a way of living that is consistent with this heritage and with their beliefs.

Photo Whiteway Archives

Basil Robert's leather-making workshop 'Makins', Whiteway. Basil and Mary Robert with other members of the Cotswold Handicrafts Cooperative. Photo date unknown, but likely 1927–30

It is impossible to disentangle Alan, his sophisticated, technically and aesthetically refined work, the life that he made with Lesley, and this pastoral, memory-laden, idealistically charged place. It is a thread that brings continuity and coherence to apparently contradictory, or even oppositional, aspects of Alan's work as an artist blacksmith and his deeply held social and political values: tradition and modernity; the rural and the urban; introspection and an outwardly directed sense of community; the dirt and sweat of the forge and the cool detachment of the digital; concern for the environment and a practice that necessarily uses finite resources and huge amounts of polluting energy.

Alan trained initially as an art teacher, but went on to serve an apprenticeship with a renowned traditional blacksmith. He became expert at reproducing leafy scrolls in an eighteenth-century style. This experience might have compounded an archetype of the outmoded rural craftsman but, by the time he finished his training, his work would be defined in opposition to his teacher. He set out to make something that was just as exact, but which was wholly responsive to the contemporary world and in which sensitivity to site would be a guiding principle.

This in turn coincided with a number of other broader shifts that were taking place within Alan's orbit of interests. Alan became an active member of the British Artists Blacksmith Association (BABA) from its inception, attending international gatherings, hosting and encouring other young makers at his forge in Whiteway and writing for the journal. In BABA, Alan found a community and a critical context for his work that emphasised making and the vital exchange of craft knowledge and fellowship.

At around the same time, the Crafts Advisory Committee, which had been formed in the early 1970s to advise the government on the needs of artist craftspeople and to promote the crafts as a field of practice, was renamed and relaunched as the Crafts Council. In the process, Tanya Harrod, in her monumental history, *The Crafts in Britain in the Twentieth Century* (New Haven and London, Yale University Press, 1999), observes what she calls a 'virtual reinvention of the purpose of the crafts'. In its institutions there was a concerted effort to distance craft from its association with the traditional, ideological positions, the rural – what educationalist and writer, Sir Christopher Frayling in an article for the January/February 1982 edition of *Crafts* magazine entitled Myth of the Happy Artisan (co-authored with Helen Snowdon), provocatively called the 'Merrie Englandism' of the Arts and Crafts movement – and to place it in relation to more urbane, and urban, contemporary visual art practices, or to the market for luxury goods.

Finding a niche in a culture that contested continuity of practice, and even values such as workmanship and fitness for purpose, was at times an uncomfortable challenge for craftspeople. Harrod describes a perception that the crafts needed to be defined and theorised in order to position them alongside other art forms as an appropriate field for discussion through the lens of cultural studies in art and design schools in the new universities. Against this background, there was a sense that the dirty business of actually making things was just a means to an end – the end being the production

Photo courtesy of Lesley Greene

Photo courtesy of Lesley Greene

Harrow Baptist Church Gates, 1983 designed by Alan Evans using the chop and twist technique, construction by Richard Quinnell Ltd.

Chelsea Gate, 1984

Photo courtesy Lesley Greene

Brimpsfield House Gates, private commission, Gloucestershire, by Alan Evans, 1983–85

of a signifying object worthy of analysis. While acknowledging that this was a part of a general atmosphere of theory in art education at the time, she asserts that craft objects already 'reified or embodied theory – commenting profoundly on the world of things and on consumption, on fine art, design, mass production and the nature of materials – visually rather than verbally'.

Whilst there was plenty of evidence, as described by Bruce and Filmer in *Working in Crafts* (Crafts Council, London, 1983), that craftspeople remained attached to making practices and, for many, even to what had come to be regarded as the ideological baggage of William Morris and his followers, the period saw some movement away from the formalist 'standards' of Bernard Leach, towards a freerer experimentalism and innovation in craft work that was evident across all disciplines. In ceramics, makers such as Alison Britton, Jacqueline Poncelet and Carol McNicol were making sculptural work that was not necessarily bound by function under the banner of 'The New Ceramics'. Similarly, in jewellery, makers such as Susanna Heron and Caroline Broadhead were making wearable and non-wearable objects.

This was the culture in which Alan and other artist blacksmiths of his generation were redefining their craft. Alan was committed to technical mastery and to function, but he embraced the sculptural possibilities of forged metal and was articulating an original visual language for metal that was of its moment.

At the same time as the New Crafts were evolving and artist blacksmiths were becoming organised, ecological thinking, which had been relatively marginal and associated with alternative and counter-cultural groups such as the Whiteway colonists, was shaping a new political movement, starting the slow process of entering into mainstream thinking. The Ecology Party had formed in the mid-1970s and was renamed as the Green Party in 1985.

Interestingly, just as craft organisations were attempting to reframe the crafts as politically neutral and coolly modern, the Green Party was keen to disassociate itself from its earlier 'beards and sandals', somewhat earnest and rustic image. For them, this meant distancing themselves from the crafts. Here is an extract from an interview by writer Rosemary Hill with the

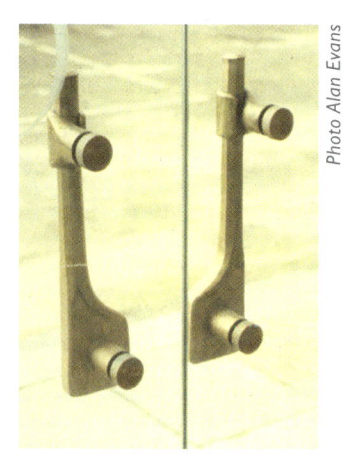

Door handles by Alan Evans for Holy Trinity Church, Brompton, London, 1986–87

environmentalist, writer and former co-chair of the Green Party, Jonathon Porritt for the July/August 1986 edition of *Crafts* magazine:

> *As for the idea of 'taking up the crafts', the Ecology Party can't be accused of that, in fact it has deliberately avoided it. We have a lot of trouble with people thinkng we're homespun and I remember that it was suggested that we should attempt to canvas craftspeople in particular, and the feeling was that, while there was probably a lot of natural support for us among them, that wasn't how we wanted to be seen.*

Nevertheless, many craftspeople had been concerned with sustainable development and had chosen environmentally conscious lifestyles that were connected to their way of working. This certainly accords with Alan's conception of his craft, which was as part of an integrated way of being. Living, working and the practice of one's spiritual, social and political beliefs were not separate, but part of a unified whole.

Alan was a countryman, interested in country pursuits – an experienced deer stalker and a knowledgable plantsman who grew most of the vegetables that he ate – profoundly connected to the landscape and environment that had nurtured him as a child. He was also active in Green politics throughout his adult life. These factors all informed Alan's work as an artist.

Forging hot metal is dirty work that requires enormous amounts of energy. It involves the burning of non-renewable fuels to increase the temperature of iron and steel to the necessary levels to be worked. Iron is a finite resource and the mining of iron ore has led to habitat destruction and environmental degradation. It also demands large quantities of water. If the relationship between the crafts and the Green Party were complicated, the reconciliation of Alan's values with his specific craft was especially challenging.

Craft implies material knowledge – not just knowledge of how things are made, but a deep knowledge of the materials from which they are made. For makers like Alan, this knowledge extends beyond specific practices and materials and could be described as a generalised attentiveness to the material world. In his seminal book, *The Craftsman* (Allen Lane, 2008), Richard Sennett wrote about craft being anchored in tangible reality. He was writing about the externally determined realities to which makers must submit themselves, including the nature of materials, the means by which they are produced and the context in which they are made. He also wrote about the craftsman as not only a problem solver, but also a problem maker: the craftsman seeks out problems to solve. In this regard, Alan both recognised and deeply felt the environmental problems that were inherent in his craft and actively embraced the challenge of mitigating them.

On one level, this meant researching and using things such as solvent-free paints and being alert to technological developments in forging that improved energy efficiency, and using recycled iron. More fundamentally, Alan believed in the principle of 'fewer, better things', making quality objects that were durable as a response to the throw-away culture of consumerism.

Although Alan was often working on a large scale, there was a certain care in his use of materials and energy which belongs to his desire to build a sustainable practice. His work has a muscular quality that is suggestive of steel and heat and force, but it also speaks of a more precise process than a forge and a power hammer. Neither energy nor materials should be wasted. The refinement in Alan's work partly reflects his design processes. For many craftspeople, making is a process of exploration in which the work is resolved through the making, but by the time Alan began to actually make something he would have developed the work with sketches on a computer using a 3D modelling program.

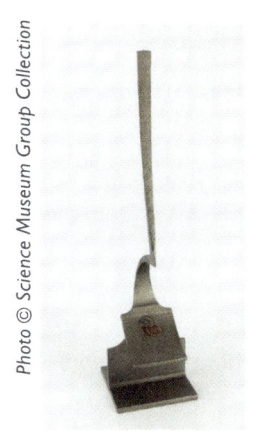

Royal Society of Arts Pollution Abatement Technology Award Scheme Trophy, 1983, designed and made by Alan Evans from scrap RSJ

Photo © Science Museum Group Collection

Through this process of detailed designing and rendering, Alan was visualising the work; clarifying and working out aesthetic and practical concerns. This careful, systematic practice carried out in the stillness of his office, is grounded in all of Alan's experience in the dirt and heat of the forge. In a long conversation that I had with Alan in 2015, he spoke of his excitement, in his early career, at the realisation of his growing mastery of his materials and processes. He described the point at which he felt himself to be inside the material, knowing instinctively exactly where to place the next blow. Forging became a regulated and controlled event, but the challenge remained in the absorbing, highly technical, complex design process where the work is imagined, modelled and finessed.

Which is not to say that the making was by any means mechanical. The making is a live event, still capable of affecting the end result. No matter how intuitive the programme, the computer can never correspond to the tool as an extension of the hand and eye; of the self. Alan was entirely committed to making. He described forging hot metal as dirty, dangerous work, that can only be done for passion. 'Nobody could pay me enough to do it!', he told me. Alan described an experience of making freely and intuitively, the sense of being out of time, of time disappearing in a delightful way.

There is a great deal more traffic between this kind of experience and the cooler, more distant activity of designing than might first appear. When Alan said that 'if I could design it I could make it', it is clear that the exchange works both ways. To say that Alan drew on his extensive craft knowledge is to underplay the complexity of that transaction. It was Alan's capacity to imagine the strike of the hammer that shaped the work and informed the confidence of his design. Although it may have been fully realised in the design process, the work is not the product of a disembodied imagination, it speaks vividly of its materiality and its making processes.

Alan's practices were contemporary; they hovered between the industrial and the handmade and they embraced both the concrete and the digital, but they were fundamentally concerned with the human activity of making and the way that making places us in the world. In this way there is a continuity between the vision that brought his grandparents to Whiteway in the early twentieth century and the way that Alan conducted himself and his practice. The concerns of the original Whiteway settlers, the dehumanising and destructive impact of nineteenth-century industrial capitalism, have new resonance as the ethical and ecological impact of late capitalist, globalised economics becomes clear. The careful placing of each mark, the slow, meticulous plotting of the design on the computer had their equivalence in the thoughtful, reflective processes of his way of living.

Gate commissioned for Painswick Friends Meeting House, Gloucestershire 1978–9, Alan Evans' first commission

ARTIST PROFILE

LISA WISDOM

The daughter of a potter and hand weaver, I grew up immersed in Cornwall's thriving craft community in the 1980s. Steeped in a foundation of tradition and skills, my parents instilled in me a sense of vocational possibility by the example of their own practice. Fascinated by making and creating, I was introduced to the medium of metal aged 11, immediately finding an affinity and love for metalworking. I quickly established myself as a maker even from this young age, creating ranges of precious metal jewellery to sell in galleries.

I left school aged 16 and spent two years self-directing my studies, taking advantage of family connections to study under many local craftspeople. I also spent several months working in France on voluntary projects, most notably participating in an archaeological restoration project in a silver mine in the French Alps. I was part of a small team of volunteers tasked with clearing silt from the network of medieval workings deep into the side of a mountain. I still look back and see this experience as a deeply affecting, pivotal moment in my understanding of the origins of metal and its extraction, and the sheer impact and scarring it incurs on the earth.

Aged 18, I experienced another such moment when I went to train as a jeweller at Birmingham School of Jewellery, where I was introduced to the craft of blacksmithing through forging jewellery-making tools. It was a hugely exciting experience and, with the alchemical transformation of the fire on the steel, a new passion was ignited. After I completed my jewellery training, I went on to train as a traditional blacksmith at The National School of Blacksmithing at Holme Lacy near Hereford and then combined further training with travel and work placements around the United Kingdom, North America, Canada and France.

I returned to Cornwall in 2008 to set up my own forge, first in a farm outbuilding, then in a beautiful old heritage smithy in the remote and overgrown post-industrial landscape of a disused granite quarry near Falmouth.

I spent several years creating large-scale architectural ironwork to commission, alongside forging a range of interior hardware to sell at shows and in galleries. I also used my 'portable forge' to gain free pitches at local events where I would demonstrate blacksmithing and sell my work.

Photo courtesy of the artist

Lisa Wisdom returning from a forage with found metal

I co-founded The Cornish Blacksmiths Collective in 2012 (which became a Community Interest Company in 2023) to connect the smithing businesses in Cornwall and to provide a supportive network for professional, student and hobbyist smiths in our area. The Collective has grown over the years and we regularly come together at local events to promote the craft of blacksmithing and to teach and demonstrate.

Photo courtesy of the artist

Lisa Wisdom at the anvil

Meanwhile, my own practice became increasingly inspired by my immediate landscape. Walking from my door, I would collect fragments of metal from past industry and incorporate them into my work, reforging and shaping the found metal into new and useable objects. Among these remnants I would find broken corrugated tin roofing sheets, once used to clad the quarry workings. These spoke to me of the Cornish landscape and I started to experiment, flattening and then drawing onto the surface of the metal with charcoals to pull out the ghosts of what I could see, be it wall or sky or building. I layered and riveted the fragments together to create pictorial, collaged landscapes. When I entered one of these into an Emerging Artists competition and won, I realized I had stumbled upon a unique idea. Thrown from the world of craft into the realm of fine art, I spent the next few years fully focussed on the development of the technique and discovering my style.

During this time, I volunteered as a trustee of The Cornwall Crafts Association, helping to promote and support craftspeople in Cornwall. I also worked part time for four years teaching blacksmithing and fine metalwork to degree students at Falmouth University. During my time there, I used the word 'artefact' as a theme and created a body of work made entirely from scrap metal and led by whatever metalworking skill my students wanted to learn that day. The artefacts I now make emerge from found, recycled and scrap metals: bronze, copper, iron and silver. They explore common forms from the bronze and iron ages such as the fibula brooch and torques, but always led by the found fragment. This time at Falmouth helped me to pull these elements back into my practice in a way that ties together my jewellery and blacksmithing background with the more 'fine art' practice of my metal collage.

Hence my career as a metalworker has continued to evolve, merging – as creative practices tend to do – with my life and landscape until all feed into one another and the individual parts can no longer be disconnected.

Trevone Quarry – where I have lived and worked since 2010 – is a nature reserve and sustainable industrial estate providing a low-impact model of working and living on the land with an emphasis on climate concern. The creative businesses here are managed by the tenants for the creation of habitat to increase biodiversity and soil health. A low carbon approach is encouraged: tenants operate a closed loop permaculture approach to all waste produced on site in the form of hot composting. They use salvaged and waste materials to renovate their workspaces and half of all travel to and from site is by electric bike. Under these principles, I have been striving to lower my environmental impact as much as possible in all areas of my life. In 2018, I decided to stop using coke and coal in my forge and explore charcoal as an alternative. This led to a fascinating journey of adapting my practice and, with funding from Falmouth University, I developed my design for a bellows-powered charcoal forge that could be adopted by the professional and hobbyist blacksmith, hoping to drive change towards sustainability. I'm really pleased to find that it has captured the interest of not just the blacksmithing community but the wider craft community too, and look forward to taking the project further.

Photo courtesy of the artist

Artefacts by Lisa Wisdom

CONTEMPLATING CARBON

Daniel Carpenter

Daniel Carpenter is Executive Director of Heritage Crafts, the national charity supporting traditional craft skills in the United Kingdom. Prior to this, he worked for Creative Lives, promoting everyday participation in creative cultural activities. He is a trustee of Arts&Heritage, placing arts in heritage locations to promote conversations about social justice, and an ambassador of the Fathom Trust, using heritage crafts as a tool for physical and mental wellbeing.

At Heritage Crafts, the British charity set up in 2010 to support, safeguard and showcase traditional craft skills in the United Kingdom, we are often met with the assumption that small artisan crafts are inherently friendlier to the environment than more industrialised processes of mass manufacture. We are always at pains to stress that it is not always as clear cut as that, with crafts such as blacksmithing, glassworking and ceramics being highly energy intensive and that do not have the benefits of some of the economies of scale enjoyed by larger businesses.

Often it is not the crafts themselves that are better or worse than their industrial counterparts, but the practices surrounding them. There can be few things as sustainable as green woodworking in a coppiced woodland you manage yourself, but if you drive an hour there and back in your diesel Range Rover and regularly fly to green woodworking events on other continents, that all has to be taken into consideration. And if there are 1,000 of you in the country doing the same thing, then even more so.

Christoph Friedrich's water hammer forge

Photo courtesy of the artist

CONTEMPLATING CARBON

Traditional crafts have the potential to be highly sustainable, and a great deal of that potential comes from removing us from many of the habitualised behaviours of global consumerism. Supply chains tend to be shorter in traditional crafts; you know at least something about the person who made your objects, and the general conditions in which those objects were made and arrived at your door. This is in contrast to the opaqueness of the processes by which cheap mass-produced products are shipped from the other side of the world, with no understanding of the distributors, wholesalers and retail chains that have been part of that journey, and even less of the conditions (both human and environmental) in which they were manufactured and transported.

But even with this nuance, it is obvious that crafts like blacksmithing, which traditionally rely on fossil fuels such as coal and propane to heat metal to forging temperatures, need to balance the moral imperative of cleaner energy with the practicality of what can be achieved with existing technology. In an era of heightened environmental awareness and the urgent need to reduce carbon emissions, they are facing increasing scrutiny over their energy consumption and ecological footprint.

The primary environmental concerns associated with blacksmithing stem from its high energy use, carbon emissions and material waste. Traditional coal-fired forges, while historically authentic, release significant amounts of carbon dioxide and particulate matter, contributing to air pollution and climate change. Even modern propane and natural gas forges, while cleaner, still rely on fossil fuels and generate greenhouse gas emissions.

Additionally, the production and transportation of metal stock adds to the overall environmental impact of blacksmithing. Material waste is another consideration, as inefficient forging techniques can lead to excess metal scraps and offcuts. More blacksmiths are looking at ways of re-using metalwork, but there are still possibilities to be explored. Alan Evans' 'Trackworks' made from recycled railway tracks and 'Metal Landscapes' created by Lisa Wisdom from recycled and scrap metal are good examples. And the chemicals used in certain finishing processes, such as galvanisation and patination, can have toxic effects on the environment if not handled properly.

Despite these challenges, many artisan blacksmiths are actively seeking ways to reduce their environmental footprint. One of the most impactful ways they can reduce their carbon footprint is by using renewable energy sources to power their forges. Some blacksmiths, such as David Hyde of Verdigris in Dorset, have begun experimenting with electric induction forges, which are far more energy efficient than traditional coal or gas-fired forges. These forges use electromagnetic fields to generate heat directly in the metal, reducing energy waste and eliminating combustion-related emissions. In addition, some blacksmiths are integrating solar panels or wind turbines to offset their workshop's overall energy consumption. Fransham Forge in Norfolk offers induction heating equipment tailored for blacksmiths, while Steve Rook at Two Ravens Forge in Glasgow is experimenting with an induction forge from France.

For those who prefer the heritage nature of a flame forge, sustainable fuels such as charcoal from responsibly managed woodlands can be a viable alternative to coal or propane. Charcoal produces less sulphur and harmful particulates than coal, making it a cleaner-burning option.

Photo courtesy of the artist

Lisa Wisdom's permaculture garden, Cornwall

Located in South Yorkshire, Gate Foot Forge uses charcoal made entirely from hardwoods sourced from sustainably coppiced woodlands near Barnsley. This approach supports local forestry management and ensures a renewable fuel source for their blacksmithing activities. Wiltshire-based Slate Hill Charcoal produces hardwood lumpwood charcoal fines specifically graded for blacksmithing. Their charcoal is known for burning cleanly and hot, with minimal ash, making it suitable for traditional and small-scale forges. In her contribution to this book, blacksmith Lisa Wisdom describes her bellow-powered charcoal forge. *(See p75)* She was awarded the Green Maker Initiative Award at MAKE Southwest in 2022.

The last working water-powered forge, the Finch Foundry, is at Sticklepath, Okehampton in Devon. It was founded in about 1800 making agricultural and mining implements, and operated until 1960. The forge reopened as a museum in the 1970s and has been cared for by the National Trust as a historic site since 1994. Christoph Friedrich, another of the blacksmiths featured here, renovated a water-powered hammer forge at Sennwald in Switzerland in 1980, which has been active producing mainly sculptural pieces. *(See p38)*

Optimising forge design and forging techniques can significantly improve energy efficiency. Well-insulated forges retain heat better, requiring less fuel to maintain forging temperatures. Some blacksmiths use regenerative burners, which preheat incoming air using exhaust gases, making their forges more fuel efficient.

Another way blacksmiths can improve sustainability is by sourcing recycled materials instead of relying on newly manufactured metal. Many blacksmiths use scrap metal from old tools, machinery, or construction materials, reducing the demand for energy-intensive mining and refining processes. This not only reduces material waste but also gives new life to metal that would otherwise be discarded. Blacksmiths can also adopt environmentally friendly finishing techniques to reduce chemical waste. Traditional methods such as beeswax coating, linseed oil finishing, and natural rust patinas are effective, non-toxic alternatives to synthetic coatings.

The question remains: in an era of climate crisis, is the energy-intensive practice of blacksmithing justifiable? The answer largely depends on how the craft evolves to address its environmental challenges. On one hand, blacksmithing produces durable, long-lasting goods, contrasting with the throw-away culture of mass production. A well-forged iron gate, tool or sculpture can last centuries, reducing the overall environmental cost compared to cheaply manufactured alternatives that require frequent replacement. In this sense, blacksmithing aligns with principles of sustainability by promoting longevity and quality over disposable consumerism.

On the other hand, blacksmiths must acknowledge their environmental responsibility and actively seek solutions to mitigate their carbon footprint. By adopting cleaner energy sources, reducing waste, and prioritising responsible material sourcing, the craft can justify its continued existence within a broader sustainable framework. We hope that the example of Alan Evans, his contemporaries, and the next generation of young blacksmiths highlighted in this publication will inspire others to follow in their footsteps.

Detail of 'The Lookout', a metal collage by Lisa Wisdom

81

ARTIST PROFILE

SHONA JOHNSON

Wow! It's hard to believe that I have been smithing for 37 years. A sideways move from agriculture in 1988 into blacksmithing has been an interesting journey, tough at times but most certainly rewarding. Many people may have thought it unusual for a young woman of 24 to switch career from agriculture into blacksmithing but it didn't seem a strange progression to me. My maternal grandfather, Jimmy Finnegan, had been an accomplished traditional smith (as well as a rifleman in the First World War), while in the 1980s my father, Phil Johnson, was developing an interest in creating forged metalwork and embracing the buzz of the revival of creative ironwork in the United Kingdom that was being driven forward by the British Artist Blacksmiths Association (BABA). Phil was hugely inspired by the International Conference on Forging Iron in 1980, organised by the Crafts Council, and had started to develop his own style of forged metalwork from his engineering business, P. Johnson & Company. This conference was a turning point towards contemporary artistic forging not only for my father but also for many British smiths of that time who attended the event.

I started working under Phil at Ratho Byres Forge just outside Edinburgh, with no knowledge of metalwork or even of how to read a tape measure correctly. However, I did have a passion for working with my hands, an appreciation of good design and an enjoyment and understanding of working as part of a team that stemmed from my days in farming. The first few years were a tough learning curve as, trained by my father, I slowly became proficient in the forge, developed essential smithing skills and explored possibilities on paper, designing pieces to be made in the forge. I became a partner in the business in 1993, taking an active role in the day-to-day running of the forge.

The skills required by the artist blacksmith are numerous, there is no end to the learning and the only way to gain further experience is by developing your design practice and craftsmanship skills. Although my basic training started under my father, my explorative training developed and continues to expand at Forge-In events. A Forge-In usually takes place over a weekend and is a gathering of smiths working together at the fire and anvil, sharing ideas and skills, creating artistic metalwork sometimes to a set theme or a set project, maybe for the local community. These Forge-In events are generally organised by BABA or by individual smiths at their own forges. Prior to social media, these events

Shona Johnson

were crucial to many artist blacksmiths as a means of keeping in touch with fellow smiths and being aware of the contemporary metalwork that was being designed and created around the country. The healthy exchange of ideas and knowledge at these events and the friendships developed with other smiths, all happy to give advice, has been – and still is – invaluable to my personal development as a smith.

Many of the smiths I met at these events in my earlier days had also taken a sideways step on their career paths into smithing and I believe that this absence of a traditional training has led to a wonderful freedom in the sharing of ideas and techniques, both in the making of tooling to create contemporary shapes and in the forging of final pieces. This friendship and willingness to share skills and ideas continues to be very strong within the membership of BABA and the global artistic blacksmithing community, something I feel is unique to artist blacksmithing. BABA, for me, is very much an international family and a huge part of my life, both as a smith and as a person. I know of no other craft where an experienced practitioner will happily share hard-learnt skills with their peers or interested students. My ongoing technical and design development as a smith has been further enhanced by working alongside and learning from my husband, Pete Hill, who is a very accomplished smith with a life-long passion for forging and tool making.

As a female, working in the perceived male environment of the blacksmith, I have to say I have never felt anything other than welcomed by the artist blacksmiths I have had the privilege to meet, both here in Britain as well as in Europe, Australia, Canada and the United States. A shared love of moving volumes of metal by forging, a willingness to embrace different forms and keep ideas moving forward with each new commission actually leaves no time to ponder on gender or strength. I have learnt that there is always more than one way to achieve the result you are aiming for. It also helps to be stubborn and just a little determined. Creating form and texture with mild steel is what excites me, heating the metal, forging by hand or under the power hammer. The material is soft and pliable while hot and can be manipulated and moved to the shapes required for each different design. My aim is for my metalwork to enhance a space; to be the ornamentation that draws the eye or has

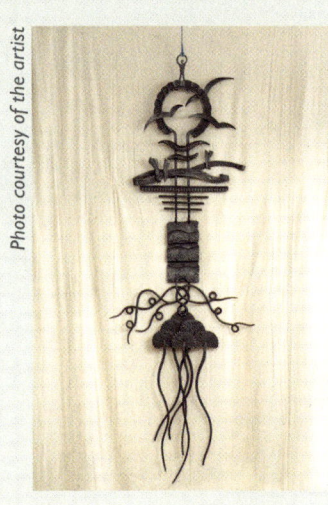

'Orcadia' by Shona Johnson, 2015

a dialogue that tells a story about the location, or maybe a historical event. I like to think that I am creating the jewellery of a space, or for a building, that will bring an element of wow and delight. Where appropriate, I enjoy introducing colour into my work either with metallic spray paints, copper or by allowing the metal to rust and develop – what I like to call an iron patina.

Photo courtesy of the artist

Shona at work, Ratho Byres Forge

As I slowly gained more experience on my smithing journey and made further contacts within BABA and the blacksmithing community by attending forging events both here in the United Kingdom and overseas, I started to feel the need to do more to promote artistic blacksmithing to the general public, which in turn would benefit all contemporary smiths through the commissioning of quality work. Most artist blacksmiths are self-employed which means, at times, we are all in competition with each for the same commissions. For me, this is never an issue because the important thing is that well-designed and well-made contemporary forged metalwork is desired and commissioned. The general public will only be aware of the craft if they see it. And the more they see, the more they are likely to want it themselves and that can only benefit all artist blacksmiths making a living from this craft. To this end, I have been involved in helping to organise various events and exhibitions on a voluntary basis on behalf of BABA, alongside many other passionate smiths who also give their time and energies to enable events to take place around the country. Not only has this led to many long-term friendships, it is also how I met Pete.

The majority of the work that Pete and I create at Ratho Byres Forge is commissioned by our clients and designed and created by both us and our team of smiths. We have developed a recognisable style over the years, with a focus on asymmetry, flowing lines, moving the volume of the material and textural forging. Pete and I tend to work independently on designs, but we will bounce ideas about between ourselves before preparing a design and invite discussion from each other throughout the design process. Once the design has been approved by the client, we draw it up full size onto wooden boards where the discussion continues on how we plan to translate the drawn shapes into forged steel and what type of tooling might be required to create the desired forms. We feel this discussion keeps the work fresh and encourages us to push our own boundaries as we challenge decisions being discussed and made. We work in teams of two or three, depending on the scale of the commission, to create the work in the forge. This enables the work to progress quickly and, again, encourages dialogue on the process of making. Employing a good team of skilled smiths enables us to create large-scale public artwork as well as our work commissioned for private homes.

In recent years, invitations to demonstrate, teach and lead masterclasses have provided a welcome opportunity for both Pete and me to push both our design and forging skills in a more personal direction, focusing on moving volume in a way that emphasises the plasticity and beauty of forged steel. Taking part in events in Britain, Europe, Canada, the United States and Australia has fostered strong friendships with many smiths from around the globe, many of whom have visited Ratho Byres Forge to attend events, give demonstrations or lead masterclasses themselves. Attending and hosting events is driven by a strong desire to promote interest in forged metalwork, both to reinforce the belief that modern blacksmithing is a viable, thriving craft and to educate the public about the wealth of possibilities that forged steel can provide in a domestic or architectural setting.

Pete and I have both been awarded silver medals for our work by the Worshipful Company of Blacksmiths, a London craft guild. I am proud to be the first woman to receive this accolade and we are also the first couple to do so. I have recently served on the BABA council as both vice chairwoman and chairwoman and found working as part of the council team to create events for BABA members a rewarding experience. I consider myself very lucky to have a profession that I enjoy whole heartedly and that has given me a massive family of blacksmithing friends who I love to spend time with, both forging at the anvil and chatting and laughing with around the kitchen table. Blacksmithing is very much my life and it is hugely rewarding on so many levels.

'Pennanular Trio' by Shona Johnson, 2015

Photo courtesy of the artist

COMMISSIONING

Lucy Quinnell

'Forging on the River' Alan Evans Masterclass 2019, Museum of Metalwork Memphis Tenessee

Lucy Quinnell is an award-winning designer-maker, curator, lecturer, writer and agent specialising in artist blacksmithing. She is the owner-manager of Fire & Iron Gallery, The Quinnell School of Blacksmithing and Richard Quinnell Ltd. (Architectural Ironworkers) in Surrey (1990–present). From 2012–20, Lucy was the editor of Artist Blacksmith *– the magazine of the British Artist Blacksmiths Association. Her recent major interests in relation to the craft are sustainability, accessibility and therapeutic potential.*

Nothing prepared the naïve younger me, starting out on my full-time ironworking career in 1990, for the tumultuousness of culture.

Three and a half decades later, still working in the same field, I often reflect on living through dramatic switches of trend both within and without the marvellous late twentieth-century / early twenty-first century resurgence of passion for creative blacksmithing.

Not for any of us the chance to keep our heads calmly down to rhythmic, sustainable work in Thomas Gray's 'cool sequestered vale'. Our technological world is fast-paced, rapidly evolving and increasingly demanding, and external events intrude universally and jarringly.

Reflection is important. One by one, the blacksmithing giants of my youth are quietly leaving the stage, exposing to the spotlight those they inspired, encouraged, trained and supported, and awakening in them a greater sense of responsibility to similarly keep this gorgeous thing – this powerful, powerful craft – going strong.

Alan Evans was a huge figure in the story of revival and influence. Highly innovative, he knew how to play with the medium of steel. He had brand new ideas, and the practical talent to match (a combination rarer than one might think).

He struck me as being like a graphic designer placed in a forge and lit up by gifts of a third dimension and malleability. The ingenuity of his designs is breathtaking, but anyone who has had the pleasure of holding an Alan Evans chestnut roaster and feeling their thumb locate into the forged depression, will also understand that this maker knew how hot metal moved, and knew how to make it move.

He wasn't 'like' anyone else, but there were edges that overlapped with some of his peers: Stuart Hill springs to mind as another clever design pioneer, as does Peter Parkinson with his exquisite grasp of the plasticity of hot steel and how that can be exploited.

I have in my stewardship a sample panel Alan made for the Treasury Gates in the Crypt at St Paul's Cathedral, and I've sat recently and looked at it – and touched it – anew. It is alien and brilliant. Captivating and tactile. The steely finish – so popular for interior ironwork today – was unusual at the time. How did this brain dream up this way of doing things? What did he see in his mind's eye that convinced him that this would work so well? And how great it is that a client was able to take such a fearless leap of faith when dealing with one of London's most iconic buildings. The commissioning process behind these gates is a happy tale of just what is possible when key figures and agencies collaborate to bring confidence to a nervous moment of risk-taking. *(See p56)*

Clients and supporters are crucial in all this. Without them, artist blacksmithing has no future. Behind every major piece of interesting architectural ironwork I can think of is a bold patron with an ambitious notion, an appreciation of the trust and free rein involved in the best collaborations, and the funds to enable such extensive work to be done. Sometimes there is also an agent – of sorts. In artist blacksmithing this role is not as common or as formalised as it is in most other creative fields (illustration, acting or writing, for example). It has usually happened unintentionally and serendipitously with a champion of the craft finding themselves playing a key agency or mentoring role simply because they know the field, see the potential and feel enthusiastic about who might be the very best fit for a particular project. These fortuitous relationships are hard to categorise or to assess, and many are based on goodwill and not commercial gain. In hindsight, it is easy to describe the evolution of a remarkable piece of ironwork and to identify all of the people who enabled it. It is much harder to prescribe in advance a route that ensures a similarly exceptional outcome.

Commissioned ironwork can be astounding. It can change the entire mood of a place and transform the experience of those who encounter it. It is tough and durable and, with the right finishing, it can last even in difficult outdoor conditions for many centuries. But blacksmithing was revived in 1970s Britain from a staggeringly precarious place on the very outskirts of contemporary craft activity, and the impetus came from the blacksmiths themselves. It enjoyed crucial support from just a very few non-blacksmith champions, and there were far too few non-blacksmithing professionals associated with the movement. It lacked the extensive network of specialist academics, writers, critics, curators, buyers, promoters, photographers and so on that surrounds those creative industries which have evolved to be more robust, more sophisticated and more accessible to potential clients. There is little clarity around the process of commissioning contemporary ironwork in the United Kingdom, and this fogginess deters. Blacksmiths have tended to insularity (albeit passionately so), and can find it hard communicating possibility, value, logistics and timescale to a wider world simultaneously less able to discern.

Wall artwork for Leatherhead, Fire & Iron, 2012   Wall artwork for Cambridge, Fire & Iron, 2022

One of my own recent public artwork commissions – in Cambridge – progressed right through the planning process before I even became aware of it. The young developer team picked a public art installation from the internet that happened to be by me (created with help from my husband, Adam Boydell and three excluded teenagers), made it the subject of a planning application, and once planning was granted I received a purchase order out of the blue. Initially taken aback and protesting that this really isn't how these things work, I agreed to adapt the unique and site-specific design for Leatherhead in Surrey and create a tailored Cambridge version. I'm confident that it has the same integrity; a replica of the Surrey artwork granted permission would have been absurd and irrelevant in a Cambridge setting, and in any case the Surrey ironwork belongs exclusively to my client. Much as I initially derided the developers' audacious method, I soon had to admit that this project was a happy one. It was well-received and all ran very smoothly indeed. I confess to feeling a little unnerved by it: if we as artist blacksmiths haven't widely imposed a lucid and accessible methodology on our potential patrons, and in a world where the nimble young are used to the internet speedily meeting all of their needs, perhaps we should welcome our produce being coaxed out of us by whatever startling means a very different generation might choose to adopt. Creative ideas are abundant. Those who can bring creative ideas to fruition in such a bureaucratic culture are uncommon. By hook or by crook, this team got its desired outcome quickly and effectively. There might be a lesson here for the rest of us.

Gates for the Gilbert & George Centre, east London, commissioned by Fire & Iron and made by David Tucker, 2023

When gates were wanted for the new Gilbert & George Centre in the East End of London, the artists approached our forge. They visited my home and I baked them a chocolate, orange and almond cake and we talked about the suitability of my

Plantagenet house for a murder mystery film. They suddenly took just a few seconds to draw some exuberant, bright green gates with one finger on a tablet and that was it – concept and design so definite and so unexpected. We knew instinctively that our colleague David Tucker, who I have represented as an exhibiting artist blacksmith in my gallery for decades, was the person who could best grasp, detail and create these curious, scribbled gates, and so it happened.

Trace most successful ironwork commissions backwards and there can be found a similarly human and untidy starting point: an informal assembly of strong characters, who have somehow found each other, grapples with vision and viability and then in each case (sooner or later) there is a sudden revelation of the best way forward. It is a process, but a semi-natural one dependent on determined, intelligent patrons rooting out those with years of immersion in a craft and its people – and often a stroke of good fortune. It is certainly teamwork. Artist blacksmiths need dynamic clients, promoters and facilitators to partner us in our belief that thoughtfulness, innovation, ambition and quality in the built environment matter.

I believe that they matter enormously. Life has changed dramatically since those energising days of the 1970s, 1980s and 1990s when artist blacksmithing was enjoying its renaissance in the West. In Britain at least, the craft undeniably thrived because of those who grafted to breathe new life into it, along with those who embraced their conviction, and we now have impressive numbers of diverse young people expressing a keen desire to be involved. This young interest is anomalous – and precious. It is the remarkable consequence of a traceable evolution with both orchestrated and organic features, and its tentacles reach not just into blacksmithing itself but into associated spin-offs such as mythology, literature, song, film and gaming. Only the most foolish of societies would let this gift of positively engaged youth slip through its fingers.

Somewhere along the line, however, the culture of commissioning brave, original and complex ironwork has suffered. It hasn't gone away, but it has certainly withered a little rather than blossomed into the lasting, lively movement we all perhaps imagined in 1978 at the founding of the British Artist Blacksmiths Association (I was young, and in the room – BABA was founded by my parents, Richard and Jinny Quinnell, at our forge in Surrey). This isn't, of course, unique to blacksmithing. It is widespread, and the most obvious parallel is architecture. With only occasional exceptions, British architecture has bowed under the pressure of capitalism to become something much more standardised and bland than it was before. Most modern buildings are designed for a neutral taste, in order that they might change hands fast, and they are built as quickly and as inexpensively as possible. Commercial viability is king. Competitive tendering ensures that the ideal people and methods are seldom used. Uniform, easy to sell, low quality and aesthetically poor buildings crowd our landscapes, exuding a demoralising sense of dull and cheap.

Façades that once commanded sizeable chunks of architectural budgets have been sacrificed as money is spent instead on mechanical, electrical and plumbing systems within buildings to meet contemporary comfort and technology demands. There is rarely scope for interesting interior fixtures and fittings made by an artist blacksmith if the priorities are low cost and neutrality. I warned colleagues in a lecture at a BABA conference twenty years ago to 'Watch your backs!' as I observed big corporations swoop on, pinch, copy and cheapen every traditional and emerging product in the blacksmiths' repertoire.

Developer funding for community infrastructure is still facilitating some significant ironwork projects, but the shift towards detached public artworks rather than visible functional structures integrated into townscapes is in many respects a shame. There is a place for stand-alone sculptures, but too often the buildings that triggered their existence are left with grim faux-balconies powder-coated gloss black and slapped across UPVC windows like a cheap child's stairgate. This is the architectural style communities are getting used to, and this low standard is all we are coming to expect of the buildings we visit and in which we live or work.

The same is true beyond the urban environment: the craze for cramming exterior artworks into every available public green space (which has been undeniably very good to us for some time) is suddenly looking tired and unsustainable. It never quite seemed right to me that close to every lauded installation could always be found a neglected run of that classily understated iron estate railing, mangled and getting stolen section by section, or an overlooked old wrought iron farm gate with its agreeable down-to-earth aesthetic held together by string. Soon these unfussy (but sublime) craftworks with their 'brown paper' wholesomeness will be lost forever – scrapped and replaced by less robust and less pleasing wire mesh fencing and fabricated tubular gates. Might a modern blacksmith restore and care for these surviving fragments of rural life instead, and make new functional countryside fixtures to an exacting design standard as required? A rustic Britain of mended fences and well-crafted contemporary infrastructure is increasingly very appealing.

Without healthier promotion, presence, flow and care of excellent, substantial urban and rural ironwork, fewer people will be inclined to commission new work and there will be ever-fewer opportunities for those so eager to learn. Blacksmithing will not survive on studio pieces and giftware alone, and the demand for those is dwindling too in a swamped global marketplace chasing an audience growing less inclined and less able to acquire 'stuff'. We need to persuade new clients, patrons and philanthropists that artist blacksmiths still have much to offer in modern and challenging times. We need to demonstrate that the process can be straightforward, reliable and hugely rewarding, and we need to do this now.

Alan Evans was a great designer-maker who has given the world an array of superb works that will enrich human lives for many centuries to come. His legacy is bigger than the objects he created, however. He was – and remains – immensely influential in our sector, and there is a major opportunity here; one which this book and the accompanying 2025 exhibition at Stroud's Museum in the Park has seized upon with such energy and vision. Reflecting collectively on this extraordinary career and this striking body of work is timely, I think, and likely to be catalytic. Big-thinking people got together almost half a century ago, concerned about the decline of artist blacksmithing. They debated, collaborated and devised a way forward, crowbarring a key craft rather spectacularly out of the doldrums.

It's time to do it all again.

Photo courtesy of Lucy Quinnell

Cara Wassenberg *'Inspired'* Award Winner 2025 for *'An idea you have not yet had time to make'*. Work in progress for *'Tidelines'* Forged from 2mm perforated, textured mild steel sheet

ARTIST PROFILE

DANE STEVENS

My journey to becoming an artist blacksmith was an interesting one. It started with a varied education and with the influence of my family, friends and creative community. My mother and nana both did silversmithing at Stroud College, in Gloucestershire. As a child, I used to sit and make jewellery with Nana for hours at a time and she and my Papa would sell it at the local farmer's market for an extra bit of money. I occasionally went with Papa to the factory where he worked as a paint sprayer to help him lock up. Looking back, this was an introduction for me to a working environment, and I found it intriguing. His work ethic was hugely inspiring to me growing up; he would be the first to open the factory at 5am and the last to leave – sometimes as late as 7pm.

I went to a small primary school in Horsley, a village near Stroud, where my mother's side of the family has lived for many years. Horsley was, and still is, a very arty community and the school reflected the community. I remember art being a large part of our learning and many artists visiting the school to teach us.

At secondary school, art captured most of my attention and I started to realise that I wanted to continue studying creative subjects when I left school. I chose three creative subjects at GCSE: Art and Design, Resistant Materials and Graphic Design. I was fortunate as the following year my school stopped allowing that combination.

Throughout my education, my teachers helped to influence my choice of career as an artist blacksmith. The most notable were Mr Davis, my art teacher, and Mr Wagner who taught me Resistant Materials. They both pushed me to achieve good grades and develop an understanding of how to work with various materials and media.

After GCSE, I studied 3D Design at Cirencester Six Form College and became both competent and confident at working with a wide range of materials. This was largely thanks to the amazing tutor, Ken. I was reluctant to go on to University, but Ken pointed me in the direction of the artistic blacksmithing degree at Hereford College of Arts (HRC). I think his words were 'it would suit you; it's hot and dangerous!'

I went to a taster day at HRC and discovered that Ken was right, hot and dangerous was right up my street. I was offered a place on both the artistic blacksmithing degree and the contemporary applied crafts degree – despite not applying for the latter. It was my

Dane Stevens

mum who encouraged me to go for blacksmithing saying, 'How many blacksmiths are there? You'll have work for the rest of your life.'

I was blessed to have the 'dream team' of tutors at HCA: Delyth Done, Adrian Legge, Ambrose Burne, Pete Smith and Chris Blythman. Adrian probably pushed me the most. He often had whole conversations with me in which he simply replied 'Why?' to everything I said. This forced me to analyse exactly what I was doing and, at times, made me realise the stupidity of my thought process. Chris had a different teaching style – he had this unique ability to teach me how to forge something while simultaneously explaining how to bake a cake or pull a dent out of a car door!

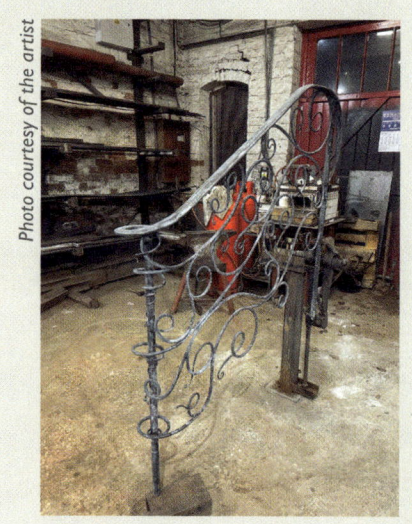

Photo courtesy of the artist

Dane Stevens, 2024

A week after graduating, I received two job offers. The first was at the bronze foundry, Pangolin Editions and the other at Ironcrafts, a small company in Stroud specialising in fabricated gates and railings. I chose Ironcrafts because I liked the idea of working for a small company. I thought I would be more involved in the full process of making a product from start to finish and might have more opportunity to demonstrate my creative side.

After a year of mainly MIG Welding (a welding process that uses an electric arc to join two pieces of metal together) and making railing panels, a friend suggested I replaced him working as an artist blacksmith for Ben Prothero. I worked on some impressive jobs with Ben, including a set of doors made entirely out of bronze and some bronze handrails and gates for Oriel College, Oxford.

I built an extensive working knowledge of bronze, copper, stainless steel and wrought iron during my more than three years with Ben, but I wanted to start my own business. I made the decision to finally take the leap towards the end of the Covid-19 pandemic and, once restrictions were lifted, my first job was to find a suitable workshop. I took the same approach I'd used to get my first job, I knocked on doors. I went to every industrial estate in the Stroud area, asked to speak to the owners and handed them a business card. Two days later, a local engineering company called to let me know that they had a workshop available to rent.

It was an old, red brick building with smashed and boarded up windows and an exterior aesthetic that screamed 'could collapse at any moment!' Despite this, I thought it was perfect so, along with two friends, Sascha and Sharpie, who are also creatives, I signed a tenancy agreement.

I had next to nothing kit wise – what I did have was bought from auctions and Facebook Marketplace – and very few of the things needed to be a blacksmith like a welder, an anvil, a workbench or a forge. Fortunately, my landlords were metal workers themselves and were able to sell me some of the key components for my trade – most of which were already in the building - for next to nothing, which was incredibly helpful for me starting out. More recently, they have offered me an array of equipment at no cost under the condition that they can still use what they need to occasionally.

My business has continued to develop and grow, and I still work and collaborate with lots of people, many of whom come from Stroud. My success has meant that I have been able to employ a local lad, Archie, as my apprentice. He wants to be an artist blacksmith too and I hope that I can teach and inspire him on his own path to becoming one.

Dane Stevens, 2023

Photo creaative.uk

ART SCHOOL FOR BLACKSMITHS

Delyth Done MBE

Delyth Done MBE is an inspirational educator and a leading international academic, dedicated to advancing dynamic pedagogy. Her commitment to developing creative craftspeople and enhancing scholarship has established a global reputation for Hereford College of Arts' forged metal arts programmes. Special thanks must go to Valija Evalds for her collaboration in writing this piece.

The value of craft, making and creativity is immeasurable, firstly because crafts such as blacksmithing carry profound cultural significance. As historian Glenn Adamson asserts in his book *The Invention of Craft* (Bloomsbury Publishing, 2018), 'Heritage craft represents the distilled wisdom of our ancestors, passed down and refined through generations.' Preserving these crafts is not just about honouring our heritage, however; it is about ensuring that these skills continue to evolve and thrive in contemporary contexts. The Crafts Council emphasises in its article, *Crafting a Future*, 2017, that, 'traditional crafts are invaluable cultural assets that connect us to our history, enrich our present, and inspire our future'. Perhaps most importantly, conserving craft also enables the next generation to flourish, personally and collectively: expanding material intelligence, enhancing our communal capacity to problem solve, supporting diverse aptitudes and approaches and inspiring an increasingly digitised, specialised world with the possibilities of making.

Photo Oliver Cameron Swan

Bran Davies' BA(Hons) Artist Blacksmithing student studio space at Hereford College of Arts

Sadly, the current school system often neglects creativity and essential skills such as making and problem solving. Sir Ken Robinson, the British author, speaker and international advisor on education in the arts, aptly noted in his 2006 TED Talk *Do Schools Kill Creativity?* that 'Many highly talented, brilliant, creative people think they're not – because the thing they were good at in school wasn't valued or was actually stigmatised.' At Hereford College of Arts, (HCA) we have many applicants who only discovered that they could make things when they were taught by a grandparent or stumbled across makers on the internet. During interviews, they mention social media influencers, such as the US-based blacksmith and YouTuber, Alec Steele, who inspired them to pursue hands-on creative work; it often marked the first time they saw someone design and create something tangible. This gap in education stifles young people's potential by not offering diverse, enriching options, and it marginalises arts and crafts, depriving students of opportunities to explore, innovate and develop critical problem-solving abilities.

Prioritising creative education is essential to nurture students' talents. Alan Evans himself attended a Quaker school that encouraged a wide curriculum and actively enabled students to do woodwork, pottery and metalworking. The approach found in many such Quaker schools, like that of Montessori and Steiner schools, emphasises hands-on work, promoting autonomy, creativity and practical skills, ultimately fostering independence and a love for learning. This approach is currently only experienced by those outside of mainstream education. The educational priorities of all schools should be revised to build an inclusive environment valuing creativity and innovation as much as academic subjects. This transformation is needed to foster a well-rounded, inventive generation.

The environment is different in art colleges, where a dynamic learning experience prioritises creativity, imagination and hands-on skills. Here students' unique talents are nurtured, empowering them to think critically, solve problems innovatively and transform materials into meaningful works of art. These institutions are essential in cultivating the next generation of artists, craftsmen and innovators. The BA(Hons) Artist Blacksmithing and MA Forged Metal Arts programmes at HCA lead the way in forged metal arts education, fostering innovation while preserving heritage skills and imparting a blend of theoretical knowledge and practical skills. They also encourage the exploration of various career paths and promote engagement with professionals in the field. Our students come from widely varied backgrounds, all united by a

Photo Gareth Williams

Joe Robinson BA(Hons) Artist Blacksmithing student working at the National School of Blacksmithing

ART SCHOOL FOR BLACKSMITHS

From Earth to Iron: The transformation of ore into metal by BA(Hons) students at *Ferrous24*

Photo Oliver Cameron Swan

shared passion for forging, often demonstrating great tenacity in finding us in the first place and daring to pursue art school for blacksmithing. Many felt disenfranchised by school education and never considered higher education as a viable option. The programme also attracts engineers seeking to break free from the rigid frameworks of their professions, finding forging a liberating form of creative expression; experienced blacksmiths looking to refine their design skills; and students who excelled academically in school but discovered a passion for forging and heritage crafts.

What does an art school for blacksmiths look like? It offers a comprehensive curriculum focusing not only on processes and materials, but also on ideas and concepts. Students learn how to forge with technical proficiency while fostering creativity and design skills. They incorporate cultural and critical theory to contextualise practice, express their ideas with authenticity and articulate their positions with clarity and confidence. The curriculum combines theoretical conversations with practical learning, offering opportunities to design the life they aspire to lead.

Alongside a robust core curriculum, there are opportunities to get involved in other learning experiences. Regular outreach projects deliver impactful workshops, such as Tools for Schools, where students take hammers into primary schools and demonstrate their art and skill. Students also exhibit work at prestigious venues such as Hereford Cathedral, Fresh Air Sculpture in Gloucestershire and New Designers in London. These experiences provide opportunities to showcase work to industry professionals, opening doors to new opportunities and collaborations. More than that, such projects involve our students in the wider project of inspiring a new generation of makers and sharing the excitement of possibility that comes with seeing an object created. This is particularly important at a time when creative and manual endeavours are so poorly supported in schools and so invisible in everyday life.

In the ever-expanding field of contemporary forged metal arts, our graduates have numerous paths to success and our programme fosters active exploration of each. Students consider various fields over the course of the programme, reflecting on their values and meticulously planning how to sustain and develop their careers, leveraging their material knowledge, skills and tools. Learning from those who have successfully shaped their lives through making is essential to this process. Early and mid-career professionals regularly contribute to the programme both online and in person, sharing their practice and discussing their values, activating and vivifying the possibilities.

Photo Oliver Cameron Swan

A piece from *the #150mm Challenge*. Ambrose Burne first conceived of the challenge for students at HCA, to transform a small, rectangular piece of steel, measuring 150 x 20 x 20mm

Historically, graduates have focused on commission-based markets, collaborating directly with customers, architects or communities to create items such as gates, railings or grave markers. However, many of our graduate's work in multiple fields, adapting and evolving their careers, and participating in various areas of practice.

Public art is one such significant field, where artists often pitch to juries to forge artworks in public spaces within towns and cities. A burgeoning market for forged metal is the gallery sector, where artists create a body of work ranging from sculptures to products. To support aspiring graduates, the programme offers multiple opportunities to exhibit artworks, paving their way into this competitive market. Conservation, a vital field outside the artistic environment, is another area where graduates can excel using their material knowledge. Closely related is the field of experimental archaeology, where objects are replicated and reproduced to generate data and support research.

Teaching and live demonstrations have also become significant paths for our graduates, ranging from higher education to hands-on experience days. These areas have grown considerably in recent years, becoming vital income sources for many. This includes YouTubers and social media influencers who share their expertise and passion for craft with a wide audience.

Community arts and therapeutic collaborations offer additional opportunities, where many of our graduates work alongside therapists to enable participants to experience the transformative power of designing and making objects.

Historically, blacksmiths have always been innovators and problem solvers and graduates of our contemporary forged metal arts programmes continue to make significant contributions across diverse fields. Their adaptability and creativity ensure their future success in public art, conservation, education and community engagement. They are also poised to make significant creative contributions to the necessary changes that face human society in the years to come. The future of forged metal design is secure in their capable hands, ready to make a lasting impact. Their material intelligence is a catalyst to a rising craft; their authentic design language transforming.

Stuart Taylor BA(Hons) Artist Blacksmithing Graduate

ARTIST PROFILE

ARIAN LELJAK

ARIAN LELJAK

It's Tuesday morning at my forge near Cranham in Gloucestershire. The two forges are gradually getting up to temperature, but the top of the fires are still a little black. Another couple of minutes will bring it up to intense orange, white hot at the centre.

Archie is checking that the three steel legs for a wooden stool are well matched before he begins to cut them to the right length. Stan is making letters for his house sign – he's going to fix them to the entrance gate – and Jed is about to fold and forge-weld his Damascus steel billet, a process that will double the layers to 160 and increase its toughness and strength. The other two pupils are making an axe and some hooks.

There is always a lot of commotion and loud chatter as we begin to settle into the work, but as the fires become white hot the mood turns quieter; it's time to hammer. As I go round trying to help the pupils structure their work, I remind myself that they are 10–16 year olds, and gently adjust my expectations.

This is one of a number of weekly home-education sessions I run and, in many ways, it is a kind of education I wish I'd had when I was growing up. I remember distinctly telling my aunt when I was 12: 'Schools should be in the forest!' I didn't realise it consciously of course at that age, but that was perhaps the moment which, over time, led me to commit to the experiential model of education; to the model where 10-year-olds get to forge hot steel on a Tuesday morning.

My approach to craft and education is informed by my early experiences. When I arrived in Britain from Croatia in 1989, I did an organic farming apprenticeship before training in sculpture. Coming from the academic and dishearteningly dry study of veterinary medicine at Zagreb University, I found tending the cows, cultivating the land, mending fences and looking after the woodland gave me a situated and experiential engagement with the substance of nature and materials – something which I went on to study and sculpt at art school.

Towards the end of my art training, a visiting lecturer came to teach us blacksmithing. Peter Pechman, from Dresden, was old, wiry, intense and spoke no English at all. We learnt by observing his body language, his passion and focus: much of it looked like a magic show. To this day, I have not found any other craft with such an immediate and graphic expression of the transformation of matter as when a hammer strikes a yellow-hot piece of iron. ('Red-hot', by the way, is a colloquialism which blacksmiths find inadequate; it represents the heat of 750°C which is insufficient for most forging operations.)

Photo courtesy the artist

Arian's workshop.

'Strike while the iron is hot' summarises the art and craft of blacksmithing perfectly. It is all about timing, focus, determination and clarity of intention. When the time is right, when the steel is glowing bright yellow and is at its most alive and malleable, that is the time to place it swiftly on the anvil and hammer it into shape. This requires calmness and conviction as any hesitancy translates into loss of heat and inefficient working.

It's when the piece goes back into the fire that we are afforded moments of reflection and planning for the next round of hammering.

I am always amazed by the contrast between blacksmithing and other crafts such as knitting. Here, a person pays seemingly no attention to their work; they chat with their friends, or even watch TV as the piece of work in front of them grows steadily bigger. Their fingers are working as fast as the knitting needles are clicking against each other, without even looking at their work! Nothing could be further from the intense visual and muscular focus a blacksmith needs to make any impression on their work.

I believe that all crafts work in two directions: outwards, as our efforts shape and structure the materials we use into useful items of purpose and beauty, and also inwards. Each different material, and their related craft process, teaches the maker about the qualities needed to become skilled – or as Richard Sennett puts it in *The Craftsman* (Penguin, 2008) '… what the process of making concrete things reveals to us about ourselves.'

This attitude was at the centre of Ruskin Mill Trust's educational approach. I worked as a blacksmithing tutor for this charity, which uses practical land and craft activities to support the development of work and life skills in young people with autism and other learning difficulties, for 20 years. During that time, I had the opportunity to go to Sweden to work and train with Kristoffer Anderson, an indigenous Sami craftsman, as well as the famous axe-makers, Gränsfors Bruk. And this was the final piece of the jigsaw puzzle: where land, with its resources and wisdom, meets Arts and Crafts attitudes, offering we humans a truly meaningful way to engage with nature, materials and the making process.

As well as home education sessions at my forge, I also work with several local alternative education providers who come to me based on their pupil's interests and aspirations. The trend towards an increasing number of young people with special educational needs and the rise in diagnoses of autism and attention deficit hyperactivity disorder (ADHD), bears witness to our increasingly complex social and practical lives.

This is a common theme for another group of individuals who attend my weekend Blacksmithing Experience days – members of the general public. Often, these people are motivated to come on my courses by a clear lack of embodied and physical experience in their day-to-day jobs. Humans have been toolmakers for over 2.6 million years so it is perhaps small wonder that increasing numbers of people are using their free time and resources to come to my workshop and reconnect with the immediate and powerful gesture of forging hot iron and leave at the end of the day with items they have made. Items which will outlast them. This is the absolute opposite of virtual reality and the fast turnover of 'stuff' that describes so much of our experience of life nowadays. As the philosopher and mechanic, Matthew Crawford, says in his book *The Case for Working with Our Hands or Why Office Work is Bad For Us and Making Things Feels Good* (Penguin, 2010), 'We want to feel that our world is intelligible, so we can be responsible for it.'

I would also argue that, in creating an intelligible item on an anvil, we also support our inner confidence and self-respect.

Knives by Arian Leljak

ARTIST PROFILE – ARIAN LELJAK

ARTIST PROFILE

MELISSA COLE

As a daughter of two teachers, the sharing of knowledge is an intrinsic part of my career as an artist blacksmith. From a young age, the influence of The British Artist Blacksmiths Association through magazines, books and events has been huge. As a young person, seeing images of the work of John Creed, Alan Evans and Peter Parkinson, among others, showed me the expressiveness of the material and the importance of design. Appreciating fine hammer work and the cleverly designed use of line and form from this forward-thinking group has kept me alert in my practice and my teaching style.

From an early age, my sisters and I were exposed to multidisciplinary making. We were lucky to have parents who valued creating art, playing and making as an integral language in our family. Our mum, Maris, was a primary school arts advisor and teacher and I witnessed first-hand the authentic approach to blacksmithing via my dad, Hector Cole, a master arrowsmith and archaeological ironworker. I tinkered in his forge, making odd things as a child and teenager. It was unsurprising that I eventually found my path to arts and education. I originally thought I would specialise in ceramics but, the moment I was away from home, I had an almost magnetic draw to working with metal and heat.

During my arts education studies degree, while developing the foundation blocks of our studio practice, we also studied philosophy, sociology (of art) and critical and cultural studies, questioning what our roles would be as artists, who we were making for and why. The crucial time that art college gives you to play and try out ideas, safe in the embrace of a learning environment, was for me a decisive juncture of experimenting with a forge that ran off a reversed-motor vacuum cleaner (a cheap way to create a fan to blow air into the forge and fuel to keep a hot fire), an anvil and a hand hammer. Traditional techniques that we as blacksmiths identify with and critique are, for me, just the starting point of my creative journey.

I learnt from my mistakes, challenging myself to create with the basics. I wasn't making anything complicated, just lines and sculptural forms. I worked with the metal flowing off the hammer and anvil, understanding how my physicality could influence the shapes, adapting to the limitations of my strength and most basic techniques. I often revert to this method of making today, not overcomplicating or overburdening myself with techniques; I just draw in space with a hammered line.

Melissa Cole, blacksmith, 2012

ARTIST PROFILE – MELISSA COLE

Hector taught me the range of traditional blacksmithing skills based on fire, anvil and hand hammer. This is, for me, the essence of the craft and the basis of my approach to the work I do. Tapers, upsets, splits, punched holes (I love a punched hole), square corners, fire welds, simple lines and forms – this is my type of blacksmithing.

Photo © R. J. Pierce

Melissa Cole at her forge, 2020

Having established that I didn't want to be a jobbing blacksmith making repeat orders, one of my first projects after graduating was to devise a community art project for a local town. I approached Southwest Arts (now ACE South West) and was brilliantly supported by Jane Bryant and David Kay. They encouraged me to use my blacksmithing skills in the project, rather than the other craft activities I had thought suitable. They valued risk-taking for young people alongside the creative skills and learning opportunities I was offering as an artist blacksmith in residence.

This project coincided with schools removing their metal work departments; the craft element was being dropped from 'craft, design and technology' and educational focus was shifting away from making with your hands. We were encouraged to be 'makers' by ACE and the term 'craft' was being disassociated from the perceived quality of work.

Taking Dad's bellows forge and tools into community groups and schools was a revelation. I didn't think anyone would be interested, but I was overwhelmed with support and encouragement. The works created on that project in 1995 are still on school walls and I have received emails from pupils I worked with who were inspired to follow creative careers having worked with me on the forge in a primary school project.

Through blacksmithing in schools, from infant, primary, secondary and specialist colleges and as far afield as JHQ Rheindahlen Primary School in Germany to speaking at a conference for art teachers, I realised that I could consolidate my education and craft skill set for the benefit of many. The broad cross-curriculum education that blacksmithing enables encompasses more than just creating; learning to look, attention to detail, accuracy of hand and eye, decision making and recognising quality of skills, plus breaking down gender stereotypes altogether, are fabulous transferrable skills for life.

As I have continued my career as an artist blacksmith, my educational journey has also evolved. From teaching a Women Into Technology blacksmithing college course and a role as short-course tutor at West Dean College, I now teach individual learning needs students (post 16 years) from my workshop in the Pewsey Vale, Wiltshire. Following a combination of my own devised curriculum and an old City & Guilds blacksmithing course, my students are learning traditional blacksmithing skills in a safe, secure environment which would otherwise be inaccessible to them. These students are supported by the local education authority and a support worker is also in attendance. One student has also received a Heritage Crafts Bursary enabling them to continue their blacksmithing training. They are also establishing a forge at home and hope to develop a range of products to make and sell.

While working as an artist in residence, I learnt that to keep the work fresh and relevant to me, I needed to let my practice influence the projects I took on. I endeavour to tie my commissions and project work to my personal thematic works of journeys, mapping and flight paths where possible. I have allowed my style to develop alongside these recurring themes in my sculpture practice; flight, journeys and paths, maps and physically remembered movement are recognisable in my work, both public and private.

The forged 'drawn' line has always been my style of blacksmithing. I approach my craft from a fine art perspective, taking on commission-based work ranging from illustrative and functional architectural pieces for public and private spaces, to the purely sculptural for exhibiting. I also embrace different mediums in my public and community-based artwork. Bronze and forged steel combined in 'Driftway Imprint' for Oxford: the Ridgeway Farm entrance sign was created following drawing and photography workshops with local residents. The design they chose reflects the landscape and history of the site and was made using galvanised steel with gold leaf detailing. A genuine love of my primary craft doesn't restrict me in my creative journey; rather it enables me to incorporate broader ideas in my projects.

I have learnt to be comfortable in the in-between worlds of craft and fine art. Importantly, it makes me question what I am doing and why, who it is for and what impact it will have on a space and its users. Showcasing the skills and development of techniques in artist blacksmithing will always be paramount in elevating the ordinary to the extraordinary.

'Percy' gate by Melissa Cole, 2022

Photo courtesy of the artist

ALAN EVANS, A SINGULAR VIEW

Matthew Fedden

After completing a degree in Applied Zoology at Leeds, Matthew Fedden undertook research into tropical rainforest ecology in the Caribbean and Africa. He worked at the University of Science and Technology, Ghana before returning to Britain in 1989. He started working with Alan Evans and now has his own forge at Lostwithiel in Cornwall.

I first saw Alan Evans' work in a small display case in Gloucester Folk Museum. At the time, I had a forge made from an oil drum, an elderly vacuum cleaner as a blower and no idea what I was doing. One of Alan's spoons was all it took. With a note of the address, I went up to Alan's parent's house in Whiteway and pestered him for a job.

The reality of working there – bouncing around in a dusty corner of the forge, holding on to a hot bar, walking down the lane on a frosty, bright morning to collect hot bread and lardy cakes from Protheroes, the local baker – was comfortable. Whiteway was a rabbit warren of people making and living together, and reminiscent of my family home. Whether it was Peter talking to the starlings that shared his workshop, or late-night designing in the 'hooter', a wooden shed that Alan used as an office and living space, this unconventional place was familiar.

The first job I did with Alan was helping to forge elements of the Brimpsfield Gates. He taught me to look carefully – a taper, a curve, an element that was out of alignment or a gate that was not in plane – and have faith in my senses. Each stage of work was examined meticulously and the final arbiter was the human eye. Alan asked all involved for their opinion, and valued it.

As the commissions became more regular, the wooden workshop, with its little forge at the side, became too small. We built the new workshop in stages, completing commissions at the same time. Alan was a great believer in good tools; when I first visited, the forge had an anvil, a mechanical sledge hammer and a kick hammer, as well as a coke hearth. As the workshop grew, the hammers and presses, lathes and forges kept coming. Computers kept coming too, because he was in love with the process as much as the end result.

The last job I worked on with Alan was a seat by a supermarket in Gloucester in 2019. When it was finished, the laser levels were put aside and I was asked to climb up and lie on top of the gantry to view the work in perspective, while Alan stayed on the ground. We discussed the positioning from our different vantage points by phone. Echoes of my first days at Whiteway, it's all in the eye.

Work in progress on St Paul's Treasury gates series, photo courtesy of Lesley Greene

FURTHER READING

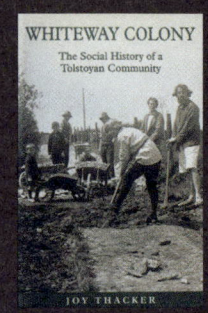

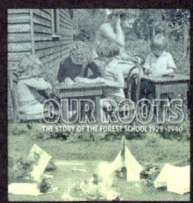

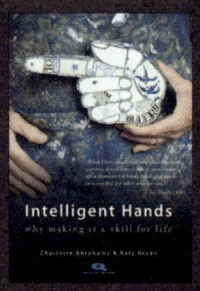

BACKGROUND:

Shaw, Nellie, *A COLONY ON THE COTSWOLDS*,
C. W. Daniel, London, 1935.

Thacker, Joy, *WHITEWAY COLONY: THE SOCIAL HISTORY OF A TOLSTOYAN COMMUNITY*,
Alan Sutton Publishing, Stroud, 1993.

OUR ROOTS: THE STORY OF THE FOREST SCHOOL 1929–1940,
Forest School Camps, www.fsc.org.uk.

Carruthers, Annette et al., *ERNEST GIMSON: ARTS & CRAFTS DESIGNER AND ARCHITECT*,
Yale, 2019.

Gordon, Aonghus and Cox, Laurence, *PLACE, CRAFTS AND NEURODIVERSITY: RE-IMAGINING POTENTIAL THROUGH EDUCATION AT RUSKIN MILL*,
Routledge, 2024.

Abrahams, Charlotte and Bevan, Katy,
INTELLIGENT HANDS: WHY MAKING IS A SKILL FOR LIFE,
Quickthorn, 2023.

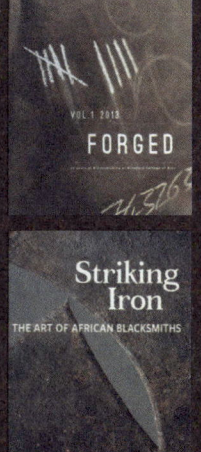

ARTIST BLACKSMITHING:

Hawkins, David, *ART METAL FORGING*, A & C Black, 2002.

Parkinson, Peter, *THE ARTIST BLACKSMITH DESIGN AND TECHNIQUES*, Crowood Press, 2001.

Parkinson, Peter, *FORGED ARCHITECTURAL METALWORK*, Crowood Press, 2006.

THE NEW IRON AGE: CONTEMPORARY FORGED METALWORK IN ARCHITECTURE AND INTERIOR DESIGN, exhibition catalogue, BABA and the Building Centre Trust, 1987

INTERNATIONAL AUSSTELLUNG, exhibition catalogue, Freidrickshafen, Germany, 1987.

Chatwin, Amina, *INTO THE NEW IRON AGE: MODERN BRITISH BLACKSMITHS*, Coach House Publishing, 1995.

Hoffman, Gretl, *KUNST AUS DEM FEUER/ART FROM THE FIRE*, Julius Hoffman, 1987.

FE: AN EXPLORATION OF IRON THROUGH THE SENSES, exhibition catalogue, BABA Touring Exhibitions Ltd, 1994.

Done, Delyth and Burne, Ambrose, *FORGED 2013: 20 YEARS OF BLACKSMITHING AT HEREFORD COLLEGE OF ARTS*, exhibition catalogue, Hereford College of Arts, 2013.

Joyce, Tom (ed.), *STRIKING IRON: THE ART OF AFRICAN BLACKSMITHS*, Fowler Museum at UCLA, USA, 2019.

Done, Delyth with Burne, Ambrose, *#150 MM CHALLENGE*, touring exhibition catalogue, Hereford College of Arts, 2021.

FURTHER READING

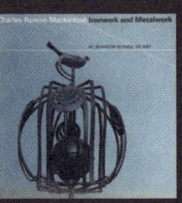

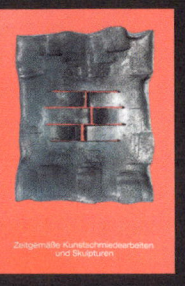

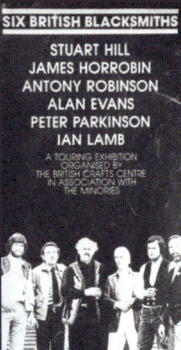

CATALOGUES ON INDIVIDUAL ARTISTS AND MAKERS:

CHARLES RENNIE MACKINTOSH IRONWORK AND METALWORK,
Glasgow School of Art, 1968, revised second edition 1978.

FRITZ KÜHN 1910–1967,
exhibition catalogue at de TiP-Galerie, Berlin, 1980.

Kühn, Fritz, *WROUGHT IRON,*
first published in Germany in 1965, second English edition Architectural Book Publishing, 1969.

Kühn, Helgard and Elgas, Peter, *ACHIM KÜHN: CATALOGUE RAISONNÉ,* Hephaistos, Berlin, 2017.

Zimmermann, Paul, *ATELIER ZIMMERMANN IRONWORK,* Stuttgart, 2019.

Elgaß, Peter, *ALFRED HARBERMANN SCHMIED UND GESTALTER (BLACKSMITH AND DESIGNER),*
German and English, Hephaistos, Berlin, 1999.

Benetton, Toni, *IL GENIO DEL FERRO,*
exhibition catalogue, Communie di Stia, 2000.

Lucie-Smith, Edward, *THE ART OF ALBERT PALEY: IRON, BRONZE, STEEL,*
Harvey N. Abrams, New York, 1996.

Merkert, John (ed.), *DAVID SMITH, SCULPTURE AND DRAWINGS,*
touring exhibition catalogue, Prestel, Munich, 1986.

DAVID SMITH,
exhibition catalogue, Tate Modern, London, 2006.

CHILLIDA,
exhibition catalogue, Hayward Gallery, London, 1990.

Fenton, Terry, *ANTHONY CARO,*
Thames and Hudson, London, 1986.

120